BACKFIELD IN MOTION!

By DON SMITH

**STADIA SPORTS
PUBLISHING, INC.**

BACKFIELD IN MOTION

FIRST PRINTING . . . June, 1973

Library of Congress Card Number: 73-80294

Copyright © 1973 by Stadia Sports Publishing, Inc., 180 Madison Avenue, New York, N.Y.

Photo Credits: Dan Rubin, U.P.I. Photo

TABLE OF CONTENTS

Introduction

By Y.A. Tittle

Hall of Fame Quarterback

■ Over the years I have very often been asked the question: What is your secret of success as a great football player? My answer has always been the same. "There is no secret."

Reaching a level of skill in football—or, for that matter, in any sport—requires no secrets or magical shortcuts, only desire, hard work, patience and the ability to bounce back from adversity. How good a player becomes depends, in a large measure, on how good he *wants* to become. The more he puts into the effort, the better his chances of succeeding. It's that simple.

I mentioned the quality of patience, and this is very important, especially for the young player who is just starting out in football. There is a great deal to learn about this game, no matter what position you play—quarterback, running back or pass receiver. It takes time! I played football for over 25 years, counting high school, college and the NFL, and I was still learning in the final game of my career. What I'm trying to emphasize here is that success does not happen overnight, and the beginner shouldn't expect it to. The greatest players the game has ever known have all had to work and wait, gaining experience and developing their skills, before attaining stardom.

Coaches are there to start the youngster along the right path, to drill him in the fundamentals of the game and to instill in him a sense of fair play and sportsmanship. The purpose of this book is to supplement that teaching and to pass along additional tips on the basics of quarterback play, running the football, pass receiving and game strategy plus special scouting chapters on the great passers, ball-carriers and receivers in the NFL. Every boy who aspires to become a good football player will gain from what follows. ●

Y.A. Tittle's passing took Giants to division titles in 1961-62-63.

It Takes Desire

■ No matter what position you play in football, or want to play, and no matter what level of the game you may be involved in—sandlot, high school or even college—there is one basic requirement that is essential to success. That basic requirement is *desire.*

Corny? Maybe it is. Trite? That could be, too. But necessary, absolutely necessary, if you want to play the game and be good at it.

Desire is where football, as a rough contact sport, begins. It must come before all else—before size and speed and strength and all the other things coaches look for in a youngster trying to make the squad.

There must be a fierce desire to work and practice, to hit and be hit, to face the challenge of football and to conquer it. No one has ever reached greatness in football without this inherent desire, this determination not only to play the game but to play it harder and better than everyone else on the field. Exceptional physical gifts such as size and quickness will help shape a boy into a football player. Only inner desire to excel, however, will lift him above the others. Good coaching, sound fundamentals and long hours of practice can help, but no amount of coaching can instill desire in an athlete. It must be there at the start, a part of his very fiber, ready to respond to the harsh demands of the game.

Quarterbacks are often referred to as the "elite" players in football. As such they are spared much of the dull routine and contact that their teammates must endure. At the same time, the quarterback—perhaps more than any other player—must come equipped with large amounts of desire. In this respect he is no different from the defensive tackle who labors in the one-yard strip of dirt called the "no-man's land" or the cornerback who faces the lonely and almost impossible task of covering the swift pass-receivers who race into his territory. These positions call for great desire.

The quarterback, even in sandlot competition, bears one burden that his teammates do not—the burden of responsibility. His brain, his skill, his execution initiate every play in the game. If he does not have tremendous desire

The late Vince Lombardi preached football fundamentals and desire.

to accept this challenge and to excel at his job, he cannot hope to succeed.

Even with desire, though, success in football—as in any other game—does not come quickly or easily. There is always a price to pay, a price in study, practice and self-discipline. There are no short-cuts. Success is achieved through diligence and, perhaps even more important, through patience. Most youngsters starting out in football (and reference is made here to the 12 to 16 age group) are in a hurry to excel. They try to cram years of experience into a single season. They quickly become bored with practice and with fundamentals. As befits their jet-age existence in daily life, they want to move ahead, to advance to the next stage.

The best advice to such young athletes is: don't be in such a hurry. Discipline yourself to learn the basics, to get a solid foundation. This can be done through study, through practice, with extra work. But it must be done. Most professional teams are composed of many great individual stars but the teams that win most often are those which emphasize basic, fundamental football. One such club was the Green Bay Packers under their late coach, Vince Lombardi. "We win," Lombardi once remarked, "because we stress fundamentals like blocking and tackling. This is what football is all about."

If you want to play football, you must also be prepared to sacrifice. Football requires a lot of time, especially for boys in junior high, high school and in college. Afternoons are taken up with long, exhausting practice sessions, and so homework and other school assignments must be done late into the night. A boy who is serious about football must also be ready to give up other social activities. He needs plenty of sleep and a sound diet. Often he must turn away from things the rest of his friends are doing because he knows it will hurt his conditioning schedule. This is what is meant by sacrifice. To play football requires total dedication and self discipline—at least if you want to be more than just an average player.

In fairness to himself, to his coaches and to his teammates, a boy must ask himself this question right at the start: Do I want football badly enough to pay the price?

If you can honestly answer "yes"—well, at least you have achieved the proper mental attitude in the beginning. And there must be no hesitancy on your part; you should make a total effort from the very first time you step on the practice field.

Because it is a contact sport, football is a demanding game. Physical punishment is an integral part of the sport and here again you must be prepared to pay a price, a price in bumps and bruises, in aching legs and tired muscles. There is no place in football for a weakling or a player with no heart. It is a give and take game and every player must be ready to mete out punishment and to absorb punishment. There are games in which a competitor can get by without pulling his weight. Football, however, is not one of them. There is no way to avoid the classic man-to-man showdown. As ex-linebacking great Sam Huff used to say, "You can run on a football field but you can't hide out there. Sooner or later you are going to get hit."

Although the aim of this book is to explore various offensive positions, you must first become a football player before you can hope to become a quarterback . . . or a halfback or an end. You will be asked to absorb and master the basics of blocking and tackling and running at the outset, long before you can devote yourself exclusively to the problems of becoming a quarterback.

Actually there should be no such thing as a specialist on lower levels of the game. A boy might fancy himself as a quarterback when, in truth, his coach will decide that he is better suited to playing offensive tackle. Sandlot and high school football is really a proving ground where young athletes are exposed to the game in general and eventually find their right positions. It must be done in this order. Experienced coaches—and most coaches at this level of the game are both experienced and completely dedicated—can quickly recognize a particular boy's talents. If it is obvious that a quarterback candidate cannot throw the ball at all but the boy shows a strong love of contact, he might be shifted to the defensive line or to linebacker where his natural talents will best serve him and the team. Again, it is a matter of unselfishness. A real football player learns to sacrifice his own desires in the interests of the team. He might long to play quarterback, a real glamour position, but if he is more effective as a fullback, say, then he must convince himself that this is the right course to take. It isn't always easy to subdue one's ambitions and desires but, again, this is part of what is meant by total sacrifice.

This is a general idea of what it takes to become a football player. It takes desire and discipline and hard work and lots of patience. It takes time; there are no short-cuts to the top. ●

Quarterback

● It has been written that pressure is the climate of a professional quarterback's life. It is a deadly and persistent shadow, stalking him in the lonely hours of the night, exploding all around him on Sunday afternoon. The great quarterbacks—on any level of the game—learn to live with pressure and to win despite it; those who do not, seldom rise above mediocrity.

Pressure assumes myriad shapes and forms in its assault on the pro quarterback. There is the physical pounding he takes from huge linemen and irate linebackers. There is the solitary responsibility for making the right decision with thousands of dollars (or a championship) riding on his call. And always there is the burden of leadership. This is what pressure is all about.

Whether he likes it or not, the quarterback in professional football is a symbol to his teammates, just as he must be in high school and college football. If he works at it he can also become an inspiration. Sammy Baugh was an inspiration. So were Otto Graham and Charlie Conerly in their time. They lifted lesser men to winning heights by the strength of their own character and by their deeds on the playing field.

The ideal pro quarterback might have Joe Namath's arm, Johnny Unitas' leadership qualities, Sonny Jurgensen's quick release, Roman Gabriel's height, Fran Tarkenton's scrambling footwork, Eddie LeBaron's sleight-of-hand, Bobby Layne's fiery temperament, Norm Van Brocklin's nerve and ancient George Blanda's longevity. For good measure he would set up screen passes with all the shrewdness of Y.A. Tittle, complete key third-down passes like Bart Starr, throw the long "bomb" as well as Daryle Lamonica, and look as good in TV commercials as John Brodie.

Since no such superman presently exists, quarterbacks will continue to be measured by the tangible factor of games won and lost and by the intangible factor of leadership. The first of these elements can be recorded in statistics; the second must be sensed or felt by the men whom the quarterback leads.

In this era of the specialist, the quarterback is the one man who cannot afford to specialize. He is required to do everything well. He

No quarterback in the game gets rid of the ball faster than Sonny Jurgensen.

must throw the football with the accuracy of a Kentucky squirrel hunter, fake with the coolness and aplomb of a riverboat card shark and feed a thousand and one facts into the computer that replaces his brain on game day. He must analyze, evaluate and execute. His decision, his signals, send ten finely-honed teammates whirling into furious action. And it had better be the right call!! The quarterback gets only one chance under the sledgehammer of pressure; there is no second guessing or changing direction once he sets his machine in motion. Retrospection is a luxury he can afford only in the quiet of Sunday night when, alone and removed from the tumult of the arena, he plays his game over and over.

Although it takes years to make a professional quarterback, his time on game day is ticked off in seconds. He races against grains of sand slipping through the hour glass. Check the defense . . . call the signals . . . take the snap . . . fake to the halfback . . . drop to passing depth . . . pick out the receiver . . . step into the pocket . . . and put the ball in the air. If he's lucky, the quarterback has four or five seconds to accomplish all this. Thereafter, he is living on borrowed time. A second longer and the defense is all over him, crushing him to the ground, maybe knocking him loose from the ball. To stand up to this pressure, to make the right call and then to execute in the face of the defensive rush, requires special talent, a talent not found in many athletes. This is why the quarterback is football's most prized article, its ultimate weapon. This is why the building of any team must begin with the men who can win under pressure. ●

Needed: A Strong Throwing Arm

■ It is safe to say that a boy must have a strong throwing arm if he hopes to become a winning quarterback. This is the one God-given requirement: a strong arm that can propel the football accurately and powerfully. If the throwing arm isn't there, the rest of the mechanics will be difficult to achieve because playing quarterback always comes down to this one act—passing the football. Ball-handling is important; so is the ability to fake. But the ultimate test is the forward pass, the chief striking maneuver in football, on any level.

In baseball, a boy can be taught to throw a curve and a slider, and good coaching can help him develop other pitches like the change-up and the knuckler that will help him win ball games. But no amount of coaching or instruction, even from the top professionals, can teach a kid to throw a fastball. He must come to the game with this ability. The strength of arm and shoulder must be there from the outset.

This illustration is mentioned because it is this way with the quarterback. He must have the arm before anything else. A quarterback may get by for a time without the ability to throw the football well, but not for long. Sooner or later he must meet this challenge. If he fails to measure up—well, he must admit to himself that maybe this is not his position.

There is no intent here to suggest that every youngster who aspires to be a quarterback must have a lightning release like Joe Namath or Sonny Jurgensen or the precision of Bob Griese or the power of Roman Gabriel. He should, however, possess the basic strength of arm that gives him at least a chance of eventually developing into a legitimate quarterback, whether it be in high school, college or even the pro ranks.

So, this is where it all starts— with the strong arm. But certainly you need more than just an arm. What are some of these other requirements? For the sake of the young players, let's look away from the professionals for the

Billy Kilmer (17) of Redskins throws "soft" pass with great accuracy.

time being and consider boys on lower levels of the game. It is, after all, at them that this book is directed.

First the physical requirements. A boy who wants to assume the difficult task of playing quarterback ideally should possess to some degree the following:

1. Coordination.
2. Height.
3. Large hands.

Coordination, of course, is first on the list—after a strong arm. The many duties of a quarterback—handling the ball on every play, faking, passing, running—call for physical skills beyond those required for most other positions. A quarterback doesn't necessarily need speed but he should have quickness—quickness of hand and foot movement and body control. Natural athletes have this coordination and reflex action. In others it can be sharpened through coaching and extra practice.

How does a young player know if he has the necessary coordination? Well, an experienced coach can usually tell in a hurry. That's why coaches set up agility drills and reaction drills in the early stages of training. These exercises give them a clue as to the skills of their players. After evaluating the results of various drills, the coach has a fairly sound idea of what a

boy's best position might be. And it is wise for young players to accept this direction—even when it means that they might have to make a big adjustment to a new position on the team. Remember, football is and always has been a *team* game, a game played by 11 men. Every fellow out there on the field has an equal stake in things, no matter what position he plays.

It helps if a young quarterback has good height. Not that he must tower head and shoulders above anyone else. No. But he should be tall enough to see over the onrushing defensive men and to spot his receivers down the field. Many short quarterbacks have made it in the pro ranks—fellows like Fran Tarkenton and Len Dawson—but it is always much easier if a quarterback doesn't have to overcome such a physical handicap. Size alone, of course, does not insure success but it does give you some kind of an edge.

Similarly, large hands can help you become a better passer. If your hands are too small to properly grip the football, it follows that you will have trouble throwing it with the right kind of spiral, and that you will not be able to control the pass or throw it for distance. Again, some men with small hands have developed their own knack of gripping the ball

Bob Griese (12) of Miami is a disciplined quarterback and a real leader.

and throwing it. As with the question of height, though, it is easier for you to master the fundamentals of quarterback play if your hands are large enough to control the ball at all times—taking the snap from center, handing off to a halfback, faking or passing.

Naturally, youngsters who are just starting out in sandlot play or in junior high competition haven't reached their full growth and thus their hands may have trouble gripping the ball. Most coaches will take this fact into consideration when sizing up their quarterback candidates. Later on, however, the size of a boy's hands will become more vital to his passing ability.

As important as the physical part of football may be, the emo-

tional or psychological side is just as crucial. Hall of Fame quarterback Y. A. Tittle, who wrote the introduction to this book, says he believes leadership ability is just as important as how well a boy throws the football. And the basis of good leadership is self-confidence. The quarterback, above all other men on the team, must believe in his own ability and he must be able to transmit this attitude of confidence to his teammates. If the quarterback lacks confidence or is otherwise unsure of himself, his ability to lead is impaired.

A quarterback can impart confidence by the tone of his voice. If it is firm and clear and has authority, his teammates will respond with confidence of their own.

Let's take an example of this to illustrate the point. Faced with an important third down and one situation, a quarterback might say in the huddle: "I *think* we can make it with the off-tackle slant." Or he could tell his team: "There's no *way* they can stop our off-tackle play. Let's run it down their throats." It's obvious which delivery would have more impact. As was pointed out, if the quarterback believes in what he is saying and in what he is doing, the others are more likely to follow him and play to their maximum.

Roman Gabriel of Rams has one of strongest passing arms in NFL.

Fran Tarkenton of the Minnesota Vikings is this kind of an inspirational quarterback, and so are Billy Kilmer of Washington and Roger Staubach of Dallas.

Leadership, of course, grows with experience. Some youngsters are natural leaders, but most develop leadership as they gain ma-

Great things are expected of Pittsburgh quarterback Terry Bradshaw (12).

Roger Staubach is unchallenged leader of great Dallas teams.

In his prime, Johnny Unitas was great passer, inspirational leader.

turity and as they improve their physical skills on the football field.

The responsibilites of the quarterback, and there are many, also include a strong self-discipline and a firm control of his emotions. If a quarterback expects his team to be disciplined, he must exercise discipline himself. He should be the first man on the practice field and the last one to leave it; he should run hard and work hard and set the pace for the rest of the team. He should approach every practice session as if it's a ball game. And he must constantly remind himself that the others are looking up to him, that his example will be followed by the rest of his teammates. Although a

quarterback's position sets him apart from the others he should always strive to relate to every man on the squad. This will stand him in good stead in some crucial game situation.

Most coaches expect their quarterbacks to be fiery and enthusiastic but, at the same time, it is important that you be a fellow who can control his emotions and his temper in the heat of a game. As the leader of the team, you must keep a clear head and not allow anger or impatience or some other emotion to cloud your judgement. This is perhaps one of the most demanding things asked of the quarterback—to be a part of the sound and contact of a hard-hitting physical game and yet to remain detached from it.

The quarterback cannot afford the luxury of becoming emotionally involved. He has too many other things on his mind, such as the game plan, recognizing defenses, remembering yardage and down situations, being aware of time left to play and so on. To repeat, this is where self-discipline is called for. A young quarterback can train himself to achieve this discipline—but it isn't easy. Each football game has a certain tempo—or at least coaches try to establish a tempo for their ball clubs—and the quarterback is the player responsible for seeing that this tempo, or rhythm, is followed as closely as possible. If he permits his own discipline to break down, the entire team may suffer as a result.

In short, temperamental athletes do not make the best quarterbacks. A boy who loses his temper quickly or who refuses to accept discipline and instructions is not likely to function well in the heat of a game, when the burden for doing the right thing at the right time rests squarely on his shoulders.

Quarterbacks, more than any other players, must also be students of the game. This is a must. The mental responsibilities are numerous and you cannot afford to simply put in your practice time and then forget about the game until the following day. There are plays to be learned, and defenses to be analyzed. There are special after-practice meetings with coaches. There are films to be studied in detail. All of these things figure in the make-up of a quarterback, even in sandlot ball where today they often do things on a big league basis.

Successful professional quarterbacks like Daryle Lamonica and Earl Morrall and Terry Bradshaw are constantly tuned in to football—no matter what else they may be doing. They never let the game get far from their minds. It would seem that these great players would know all there is to know about their position and about the game, and yet they never stop studying and learning.

Because of the many demands made by his position, the quarterback—especially those still playing on the school level—should make a strong effort to organize his time. It is wise to set up a schedule of school, study and practice activities, either by the day or the week. This way, a young player can get the most out of his school and practice hours. As mentioned in the previous chapter, this often means sacrificing things that a boy likes to do but, again, the price is high if you want to play quarterback. ●

Start At The Beginning

■ Playing quarterback is like doing anything else in life. If you start correctly, your chances of success are better than if you get off, as they say, on the wrong foot.

With this warning in mind it is good to consider here some of the fundamentals of quarterback play.

Although many different styles and variations can be seen in the play of top quarterbacks in professional and college football, most of them are careful to observe the proven mechanics of the position—things such as stance, body position, hand position and receiving the snap. These are fundamentals that rarely change, and so it is sound advice for a young quarterback to learn them and practice them right from the start—before he gets into bad habits that will affect his play later in his career.

The first thing a quarterback should seek from his basic body position (or stance) is comfort. A relaxed, comfortable starting point makes it easier for the body to react and to make subsequent moves. A tense, awkward posi-

tion, on the other hand, almost rules out ease of movement when the ball is snapped.

In the standard T-formation, the quarterback stands behind the center with his feet spread com-

Quarterback's overall body position is firm but relaxed.

fortably apart (but seldom wider than the shoulders). The idea here is to achieve good balance and at the same time to allow for quick, easy movement once the play starts. The body is in basically an upright position but the knees should be slightly flexed. The position of the feet varies with different plays but usually the quarterback lines up with the toe of one foot opposite the instep of the other foot. Some coaches advocate a toes-even stance but this is not really that important at this point. Slight adjustments can always be made once the fundamentals have been mastered.

It might help young quarterbacks to think of the overall body as *firm* but *not tense.*

If the center is tall—that is, if he has long legs—the quarterback may need a slight forward bend to put his body in the best position to receive the ball on the ex-

Front view of QB stance shows feet at shoulder width, head up.

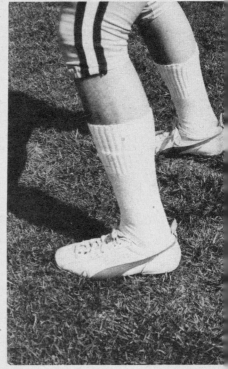

Close-up of stance shows proper alignment of feet and bent knees.

QB positions his shoulders over center's hips prior to snap.

QB keeps head high, shoulders square during center exchange.

change. A good check is to have the shoulders line up over the center's hips; this usually indicates the two players are in good alignment. In all cases, the quarterback must keep his head up. If he is lined up correctly over the center, there is no reason for him to have to look down. The ball will be there on the snap. He doesn't have to see it; he can feel it. Meanwhile, with his head high, the quarterback can scan the rival defense as well as check the position of his own players.

The positioning of the quarterback's hands under the center's tail is important because this is where it all starts—with the ball

exchange between these two players. An error here, even one of a few inches, can destroy the timing of a play and, even worse, lead to a costly fumble.

In the T-formation, the quarterback places his passing hand (usually the right) with the palm facing the ground and the back of the hand resting firmly against the center's butt. The fingers are extended and they exert a continual pressure on the center. This pressure, incidentally, is a reassurance to the center that the quarterback is there in the right position and ready to receive the snap.

The left hand (or bottom hand) is positioned with the heel

of the left palm touching the heel of the right palm. The bottom hand serves as a "trap" for the ball when it is centered. In other words, it helps form a cup with the right hand into which the center slams the ball on the snap. There should never be a gap at the point where the two hands are joined; they should almost be "hinged" together.

Good quarterback play depends largely on precision teamwork with the man centering the ball. There must be smoothness and coordination during the exchange—or everything that follows is apt to be out of synchronization. This means one thing to all quarterbacks and centers—PRACTICE. Hours and hours of routine, boring practice. Hundreds and hundreds of snaps until perfect teamwork and "feel" has been achieved. This is something you will see on every level of the game—quarterbacks and centers off to one side of the field working to perfect the all-important exchange.

Not all quarterbacks are built the same; nor are all centers the same. There are differences in size and reaction and reflex, and so the two men must get to know each other through constant drilling. Centers vary on their stance and with the action of the snap itself. For example, one center

Back (top) of right hand presses firmly against center's butt.

Left hand serves as "trap" for ball during the exchange.

*This is the correct position
of hands to receive the snap.*

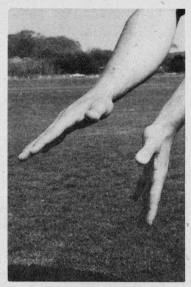

*Never leave gap between hands
(as shown here) on exchange.*

might be quicker than another getting off the mark on the snap signal. This means the quarterback, aware of his teammate's fast getaway, must move his hands slightly forward on the snap to make sure that he "stays" with the ball despite the center's movement. Only conscientious practice will achieve this timing. During this practice, the two men can also get used to the quarterback's cadence—calling signals—but this will be discussed later.

Most quarterbacks like to take the snap so that their passing hand—or at least the fingers of the passing hand—is across the laces of the football. This is another part of the quarterback-center teamwork that requires lots of practice. If the passer is righthanded, as is usually the case, the center places the ball on the ground and positions his right hand (the hand that will actually deliver the snap) opposite the laces. In this case, the center's left hand will be touching the laces. When the center snaps the ball sharply with his right hand, the laces should hit directly into the fingers of the quarterback's right hand. Again, constant practice between these

Rear view of quarterback's hand position prior to snap from center.

1—Starting position as center prepares to execute one-hand snap.

2—Right hand brings the ball up and starts turning it.

two men is the only way to insure that the quarterback receives the ball properly *every time.*

Since no play can hope to succeed if there is a bad exchange or a fumble on the snap, the importance of a good exchange cannot be over-emphasized. It is important that the quarterback always reach out, so to speak, to get the ball from the center. And in order to reach out, it is necessary for the quarterback to have most of his weight on the front foot. As he shoves off—or pushes away—with this front foot, his hands will automatically move forward. It will also help if the quarterback learns to take a small backward step on every exchange. By taking

3—*Laces are now ready to hit quarterback's passing hand.*

4—*Completion of the snap with laces in right position for QB.*

this small step with the back foot, the weight is automatically shifted onto the front foot. This shift of weight makes the quarterback's hands "dip in" to get the ball.

Although many of these tips on basic quarterback stance while receiving the snap may seem mechanical in the beginning, a good deal of practice will make them become almost automatic in time. The quarterback will assume the proper stance, body and hand position without even thinking about them. They will become part of his natural movements.

When the beginning quarterback has reached this stage, he is then ready to consider the next problem: starting the play. ●

Handling The Football

■ The center has made the snap. You have the football. What now? Starting the play *correctly* is vital to completing the play successfully.

Whether the play is to be a run or a pass, your first move after taking the snap is to bring the ball into your body at belt buckle level immediately. There are three reasons for this, each one as important as the others:

1. All handoffs and pitchouts to offensive backs are delivered at belt buckle level, so it is important to have the ball there from the start of the play.

2. Bringing the ball into the body lessens the chance of a fumble, or of having the ball knocked loose by one of the offensive linemen who may be pulling laterally down the line to block on a running play.

3. Deception is better if the defense cannot see the ball right away. By keeping the ball close to his body, the quarterback hides it—momentarily, at least—from the view of the defense.

It might appear that much of this material is fundamental to the point of being unnecessary but it should be pointed out again that no fundamental in football is too simple to consider and to apply. Great professional coaches like Paul Brown of the Cincinnati Bengals and top college mentors such as Darrell Royal of the U. of Texas all preach the doctrine of fundamentals before everything else.

Once you receive the snap from center you must put yourself into motion. If you intend to pass, you start your backward pass drop; if you have called a running play, you must spin (or pivot) to make the handoff to one of your running backs. In each instance, your initial responsibility is to get going.

Footwork, naturally, is vital to playing quarterback. And the push-off away from center requires this footwork. Here's how it works: you raise the heel of the foot closest to the center and give a quick push off the ball of this foot. The knee is slightly flexed but it is not bent. With the weight

Jets' Joe Namath shows classic form as he prepares to hand off.

QB turns head and shoulders as first part of spin away from center.

Ball is pulled into belt buckle as QB moves away from center.

forward on the foot nearest the line of scrimmage, you can use it almost like a spring.

Another advantage of placing the weight on the front foot is that this has a tendency to make you keep your hands under the center's tail for a split second longer, thus reducing the possibility of a fumble if the center drives off the mark too soon.

There is one important thing to remember about spinning away from the center at the start of the pivot: start the spin by turning your head and shoulders first. In other words, turn from the waist up, throwing the head and the shoulder in the direction you want to spin. By twisting from the hips up, it is not difficult to turn your head and shoulders. This gives you a chance to see your backs and to make any spacing adjustments that might be necessary.

There are many different mechanics involved in the act of pivoting with the feet—too many to cover here. One basic rule that stands up, however, is this: the front foot is the direction foot, while the rear (or back) foot is used to pivot on. If the direction of your pivot is to the left, you step forward with your left foot first, then with your right foot if another step is needed. Similarly, if the direction of the pivot is to the right, you step toward that spot with the right foot leading the way.

As mentioned, there are numerous types of spins and pivots and they depend on the kind of play that has been called. As with other aspects of quarterback play, these pivots can best be learned by constantly retracing the steps in practice until the footwork becomes automatic.

The exchange between the quarterback and the ball-carrier is every bit as vital as the exchange between quarterback and center. The quarterback is the link between the two. He is responsible for continuing the movement of the ball from center to running back.

It has been said that two-thirds of the responsibility for a smooth handoff rests with the quarterback and one-third with the man receiving the ball. Most quarterbacks, though, prefer to assume the *entire responsibility.* True, this puts more pressure on the quarterback but, as has been pointed out earlier, pressure is the climate of a quarterback's life. If, as the quarterback, you think in terms of *giving* the ball to the backfield man instead of having him *take* it from you, you have only yourself to worry about and not the other man too. This narrows down the area of possible errors on the handoff.

After making your pivot and moving to the point of the handoff (which differs with various running plays and formations), you should pick out a spot on the receiver—say, his belt buckle—and keep your eye on that spot until the exchange is completed. By drawing a bead on this spot you are always able to make last-second adjustments on the handoff. Sometimes the back might veer in too close to you; other times he may go too wide. In any event, it is your job to *get the ball to him.*

While on this subject, it might be wise to mention that the quarterback must know the character-

QB must place ball in runner's mid-section, not slam it in.

istics and physical traits of all his running backs, just as he must know the moves of his receivers for the passing game. Some backs hit in there hard on the handoff; others come in at three-quarter speed and then accelerate after taking the handoff. You'll find one back is faster off the mark than the others and this means you have to make your pivot much quicker in order to get the ball to him before he's by you and into the line. Each back is different and it is the quarterback's job to be aware of these differences and be prepared to compensate for them.

Size is a factor, too. It requires a slight compensation sometimes to get the ball to a taller back who comes into the line straight up, or to a smaller, chunkier back who bends low to the ground as you make the handoff. Some backs have better hands, a better "feel" for the ball during the exchange, and this too is a factor for the quarterback to consider.

It has been debated at length whether the exchange should be made with two hands on the football or just one. In the long run, it is probably a matter of style. High school coaches often prefer two hands on the ball because this reduces the incidence of fumbling. In most cases today, though, the exchange is made with just one hand, primarily because it is

During exchange, QB keeps his eye on spot where he wants to place ball.

"Riding" the ball as runner takes handoff from quarterback.

easier, faster and a lot more natural. For example, if a ball-carrier runs wide of the quarterback, it is simpler for the quarterback to stretch out with one hand and reach him with the ball than it would be to stretch both arms.

Usually, the ball is exchanged with the same hand and the same foot. This means that if you give the ball to the halfback with your right hand, then your right foot will be closest to that man on the handoff. This helps maintain better balance and keeps your body between the ball and the defense for better deception. The smoothest handoff is achieved when the "giving foot," or nearest foot, is planted firmly on the ground just before you begin the actual exchange. This enables you to de-

If runner veers too wide, QB must use long one-hand stretch on exchange.

NFL quarterback shows perfect form for underhand pitchout to halfback.

liver the ball smoothly and sharply and with a solid base.

The ball should be placed in the receiver's mid-section, not slammed in there. The best way to avoid a sudden jolt during the exchange is for the quarterback to "ride" with the blow—that is, after placing the ball, you let your hands give about six inches, something like the action of a shock absorber.

Faking is a part of quarterback play but it is always secondary to the primary object of getting the ball to the running back on a handoff or pitchout, or dropping back to throw a pass. A fake can *help* a play but it rarely *makes* a play. If you want to become a good quarterback, use the fake but don't depend on it too much or too often.

Faking a handoff to a back rushing into the line increases the danger of a fumble, so always

think in terms of "safety first." Make the fake, if the play calls for it, but don't risk loss of possession of the ball in the interest of deception.

All fakes must be made briskly and with the quarterback always keeping firm control of the ball. Don't stick the ball out there loosely with one hand—or the decoy back may knock it out of your grip and spoil the whole play. Thrust your hands into the faking back and then pull the ball back to your stomach again before making the exchange with the real ball-carrier. Arm and hand fakes are usually only partially effective. More often you can add to the deception by merely dropping (or dipping) the shoulder nearest to the faking back. To the defense, this dipping move might resemble the actual handoff motion.

Remember that you must always carry out your fakes on a given play. If you actually give the ball to the first back coming through, be sure to make the fake to the second man (the decoy) as realistic as possible. Far too often young quarterbacks relax after making the handoff and the fake is meaningless. Carrying out all fakes is valuable in setting up future plays from the same sequence.

There are two methods of getting the ball to your backs on running plays. One is the handoff, which we have just discussed. The other is the pitchout. The pitchout can be made with one hand or with two hands (the old basketball pass, as they call it). Most quarterbacks today prefer the one-handed pitchout for the reasons that it is faster, easier and gives them better control of the ball during the actual delivery.

The pitchout, of course, is used for wide running plays, end runs, sweeps, etc. Its purpose is to get the ball to a wide-running back in one swift motion. It is risky because it involves precise timing and teamwork between you and the ball-carrier.

Here's how you execute the pitchout. Take the ball from center and spin immediately in the direction of the receiver, keeping your knees flexed, your body low and holding the ball on the side you are going to pitch it from. Your body and the point of the ball face your target directly. The foot opposite your passing arm is forward. It is your direction finder and you will throw off that foot while delivering the ball. With your eyes following every move made by the receiver and your body kept low, you swing your throwing arm in an underhand motion and release the ball. Again, the belt buckle is your target. You want to keep the ball on a flat plane—that is, you don't want to arch it like a forward pass. As always, it is important to follow through. Your fingers, hand, arm and head should all point directly toward the target as you complete the pitchout motion. You actually extend your body along the same line of flight taken by the football.

Since pitchouts—as well as laterals—require such precise timing, you should spend as much practice time as possible on this phase of quarterback play.

In fact, all of the quarterback mechanics discussed in this chapter require considerable practice. Each one is important if you are to master all the fundamentals required to become a top quarterback. Review them often—and practice, practice, practice! •

Detroit Lions quarterback places ball in runner's mid-section.

Putting It 'In The Air'

■ Throwing is second nature to most American boys. Youngsters who have never been taught the mechanics of throwing will pick up a baseball or football or even a rock and toss it smoothly and flawlessly. But even though you have this inbred ability you can't hope to become a passer until you learn to combine your natural talents with the proven fundamentals of throwing a football.

The forward pass, naturally, starts with the grip. If the ball is not held properly at the outset, it can hardly be delivered properly. So, learning the right grip is your first order of business.

If the center does his job on the snap, you should receive the ball with the fingers of your right hand extended across the laces and the left hand cradling the underside of the ball. The left hand serves as a guide and a support until the ball is brought into position for the actual delivery of the pass.

All good passers have a sensitive "feel" for the ball—and this is achieved by holding the ball in the fingers of the right hand and not in the palm. Feel is experienced through the fingers. This is true in almost every other sport, too—in baseball, hockey, golf and tennis.

The ball is gripped about one-third of the way down from the end (or rear point) with the fingers spaced comfortably and naturally across the laces, and the thumb serving as a brace underneath. The control finger of the passing grip is the index finger. It acts as a directional guide since it is the last finger to leave the ball as it is released. The index finger aids in keeping the nose of the ball level. You don't want the nose of the ball pointing up or down; you want it level, which gives you a better spiral and more distance.

The pass drop technique varies with individual coaches, formations and the physical ability of the quarterback. There are various methods of dropping back. You can use the cross-over step or the straight back-pedal or even the

The passing grip: fingers spread comfortably over laces.

Left hand helps support (or cradle) ball prior to release.

sprint-out. The main point on the pass drop, no matter which style you prefer, is to get back to your passing depth (usually about seven yards) as quickly as possible with your body under control. There's no sense dashing away from the center in the interest of speed if your moves are not smooth and coordinated.

Good footwork, as always, is vital to a coordinated pass drop. You must get back there in a hurry and set up on a solid base—

and this requires keen footwork, not out and out sprinter speed. Most top quarterbacks have what coaches like to call "live feet." This doesn't necessarily mean they are fast runners; rather it indicates that the quarterback can move quickly and with complete body control in a given area of play.

Time is essential on the pass drop. Fractions of seconds can make a big difference in a ball game. So practice your drop whenever possible. Work for quickness but also be certain to make your drop under control. This cannot be emphasized too much.

Once back to your passing depth, you must set up to throw. There are points here that must be mentioned, too. The weight must be kept on *the balls of the feet,* not back on the heels. If you are a righthanded passer, your left foot points toward the target and your right foot (the rear foot) is planted firmly at a 90-degree angle, giving you a base from which to push off as you move forward into the throw. Be sure to keep your head up and your eyes open. Never look down at your feet (That's why it's important to practice your footwork until it becomes automatic!) or at the ball. You can tell if you have the right grip by the placement of your fingers across the laces. This is what's meant by "feel."

As you move away from the center after taking the snap, hold the football close to your stomach with both hands, the right hand and fingers on the laces and the left hand under the ball. When you start the passing motion, use both hands to bring the ball up toward your right ear. The left hand acts as a guide during this move and, at the top, the right hand takes control of the ball.

Many coaches advocate bringing the ball up to shoulder level as soon as it is received from the center. The theory here is that this will save the quarterback time when he reaches his passing depth; he will already have the ball up high when he gets back there.

Both hands should grip ball as quarterback starts pass drop.

QB uses cross-over step (above) to get back to passing depth.

Some pro quarterbacks, however, disagree with this rule of thumb. Fellows like Sonny Jurgensen, the Washington Redskin great, hold the ball low all the way back and they don't make a separate movement to bring it up to shoulder level. They simply go into a natural throwing motion and the ball is raised to the right level automatically.

To build up momentum for the pass, swing your right arm and right shoulder around so that your left shoulder is facing the target. The left foot should also be aimed at your intended receiver.

As you begin the actual throwing motion, step forward onto the left foot—directly toward the target. With the weight shifting forward onto the left side, you then swing the right arm, shoulder and hip into the throw, uncocking the wrist at the last second and allowing the ball to roll off the finger-

Weight is on the balls of the feet as QB sets up to throw.

QB uses left foot as directional foot, with weight on rear leg.

tips. This gives you maximum control.

The quarterback's role in the pass is not finished when he releases the ball. You must then follow through by extending your right arm and shoulder—indeed, the entire right side—along the same path the ball has taken. This is sometimes known as throwing "through the ball." Check your position at the completion of the follow-through. If your right hip and right shoulder are pointed toward the target, you have finished the throwing motion correctly. If your body is not in this position, however, you have not followed through the way you should.

The accepted method of delivering the forward pass is with a straight overhand motion similar to a baseball catcher throwing down to second base. By throwing overhand, the passer has better

Pass should be delivered with full overhand motion of passing arm.

Right arm follows through toward target as weight shifts forward.

control of the ball and gets more accuracy and distance. However, this does not mean that a pass cannot be thrown three-quarter overhand or even sidearm. Some of the game's great passers have been sidearm throwers. Coaches would be wise not to change a boy's style if he happens to be a sidearm passer. This kind of motion may restrict him on certain types of passes but, at the same time, the sidearm delivery can be more effective on other types of passes. The main thing is to *complete the pass,* no matter how you throw it.

The passing techniques described here apply primarily to the standard drop-back passer who throws from the protective pocket. Today, of course, there are many quarterbacks who throw from the sprintout or rollout formations, which means they are throwing on the move and cannot possibly set up as outlined in this chapter.

Not every quarterback is equipped to handle the sprint-out or rollout pass. This maneuver requires a very strong arm, exceptional balance and a quick release. Because he is forced to pass in a moving pattern, the rollout passer is unable to set up in a pocket. He can't throw off a solid base and thus he must rely on wrist action alone to propel the ball downfield. Under these conditions it is often difficult to achieve both accuracy and distance.

For the young quarterback, then, it is better to concentrate on the standard pass drop in the beginning. Work on the mechanics of getting back quickly, setting up properly and releasing the ball with a good follow-through. There will be time later to worry about rolling out, sprinting out and, yes, even scrambling like Fran Tarkenton or Roger Staubach.

Redskins' Sonny Jurgensen (9) plants right foot as he sets to throw.

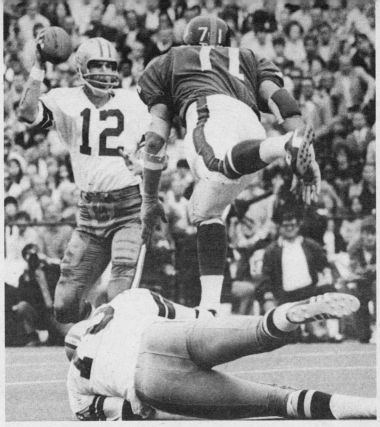

Roger Staubach (12) of Dallas keeps eyes on receiver despite pressure.

As you gain experience in passing, you will discover that certain types of passes must be thrown differently than others. For instance, a hook pattern or a quick sideline route requires a quick, hard throw. If the receiver is running diagonally across the field, a softer, easier-to-handle ball is required. On long patterns, the ball must be floated high, giving the intended receiver plenty of lead time—that is, throwing the ball ahead of him and letting him run under it for the catch. Screen passes and flare passes to backs circling out into the flat demand a precise touch by the passer.

All of these passes will be easier for you to throw if you take the time in the beginning to master the fundamentals of taking the snap, dropping back, setting up and releasing the ball.

And remember, there are no shortcuts. To become a good passer, you'll have to work twice as hard as anyone else. ●

Think Like A Quarterback

■ It has been said that good quarterbacks *think* they can complete every pass they throw while great quarterbacks *know* they can. This, of course, is an over-simplification of the case but it does serve to point up the importance of confidence in the make-up of a quarterback. This is no position for a negative thinker.

Naturally, no quarterback completes every pass he attempts, just as no baseball player gets a hit every time at bat and just as no basketball player makes two points every time he shoots. The top quarterbacks, though, are often able to psyche themselves up so that they believe anything is possible.

Joe Namath of the New York Jets is such a player. Regarded by many as the best passer in football today, Broadway Joe is never gripped by self-doubt. He always believes in his own ability to complete the pass. He is supremely confident—a confidence that is often mistaken for arrogance and cockiness. But without this confi-dence—or self-assurance, if you prefer—Namath might be just an average passer instead of a brilliant one.

This trait is common not only to modern quarterbacks. It has always been the trademark of the great passers.

There is a story about the redoubtable Sammy Baugh's first day as a rookie in the training camp of the Washington Redskins. Coach Ray Flaherty, anxious to learn if his new quarterback was as great as they said he was, told Sam:

"Wayne Millner here is gonna run a buttonhook over the middle, and I want you to hit him right in the eye with that football. Right in the eye, understand?"

"Yes, suh," drawled Sammy, "but just one question, coach?"

"Yes?"

"Which eye?"

Whether young Samuel Adrian Baugh, fresh out of T.C.U., ever hit Millner in the eye is unrecorded. But Sammy did prove one thing that first day as a pro—he

Confidence makes Joe Namath of the Jets a great all-around quarterback.

had no doubts as to his ability to throw a football.

This is the way it should be with every young man who aspires to be a quarterback. You must be confident, sure of yourself, unafraid to put the football in the air.

There is a certain risk involved in throwing the ball. Four things can happen when you "put it in the air," as Y.A. Tittle used to say—and three of them are bad. One, it might be intercepted. Two, it might be batted down or dropped by the receiver. Three, you might be thrown for a loss of yardage while trying to pass. And four, you might complete it.

This means the confidence in your ability to throw a pass must be tempered by sound football thinking plus a little old common sense.

There is a time to throw the ball, and there is a time *not* to throw the ball. There are certain types of passes which should be thrown, and others that should *not* be thrown. These are determined, in most cases, by such factors as the score, the time remaining to be played, yardage and down situation, field position, weather conditions, the offensive game plan, injuries and, of course, the defense you are playing against on a given day.

Before you throw the football, many of these factors must be considered. They will determine your decision. This is the burden of responsibility you face as the leader of your team. There are dozens of options available on any given play—and you are expected to select the right ones. This is why the quarterback exists in a climate of pressure.

Effective passing strategy, then, begins in the quarterback's mind. *Constant thinking* is another way of saying it. You must stay on top of the game all the way. You must remind yourself of the options and run them through your mind before you make your decision in the huddle. You can never afford to relax mentally; other players enjoy this luxury, but not the quarterback!

During a timeout or in the brief interval between plays, a good quarterback asks himself a hundred questions and tries to answer them in his mind.

"How deep are those defensive backs playing? Is the wind too strong to go deep on the next play? Which pass pattern has been working best against them today? Can my line give me the protection I need for a long bomb? Are they double-covering my split end? What worked for me last time on third and six? Should I call for a multiple pattern (three or four receivers going out) or

Fran Tarkenton (10) is an inspirational leader on football field.

keep my backs in to block? Am I too close to that right sideline for a quick square-out pattern to the flanker? Are those linebackers going to blitz? If so, should I try an outside screen?"

Experience will help you handle these many problems on the field. Meanwhile, train your mind to focus constantly on the game and everything about it. Don't go to sleep out there and expect to do it all with your arm.

The successful quarterback is the one who knows how to get the best results out of his personnel. This is why it is important to study your teammates and familiarize yourself with their strengths and weaknesses. Some receivers, for instance, can catch the ball going away but are not good at catching it when they have to stop and turn around to face the passer. Homer Jones, the great split end of the New York Giants a few years ago, was like this. Homer could catch anything deep down the sideline or in the long zones over the middle but he had difficulty running a button-hook route where he had to receive the ball while standing still. Consequently, quarterback Fran Tarkenton rarely called a button-hook play for Homer. He went to Jones' strength, not his weakness.

In time, you should be able to recognize what your receivers—and also your running backs—do best. You will find, for example, that one of your ends is exceptionally strong and can catch the ball on those short routes over the middle where the linebackers get pretty rough on pass receivers. He's your man on third and three, when you *have* to put it in the air but when you don't want to go deep. Another end may be particularly adept at the square-out pattern, while still another may be fast enough to run the deep routes. Use these players on the patterns that they do best. It will help the team effort—which is your primary responsibility—and it will make you a more successful quarterback.

Another thing—avoid the mistake of "playing favorites." That is, don't throw too often to one man because he is an off-the-field friend or because he may be the best receiver. Use all of your personnel. Mix it up. Keep the defense guessing. Always keep in mind that winning football is a team game, an 11-man game, and *individual effort should only be part of the overall team effort.*

In the beginning, the young quarterback should rely mainly on the advice of his coach and on the game plan for a particular day. Your coach is an experienced football man and in all probability he has been through it all himself. He is aware of the many problems facing a young quarterback, and his suggestions will prove very helpful to you once the whistle blows.

Many novice quarterbacks fall into the trap of trying to do it all with the pass. It's good to have this confidence, as has been repeated time and again, but it isn't sound football when you ignore the other offensive weapons at your disposal. Keep this one fact in mind: seldom is a passing attack highly successful if the running game has not also been effective! Most college and professional teams aim for a balance between running and passing; this is the ideal strategy for a successful attack. It doesn't always work this way, of course, and often a team

Bill Nelsen (16), Cleveland quarterback, is another fine leader.

is forced to put the ball in the air more than it had planned to. This is part of football; rarely does everything work the way the coaches diagram it on the blackboard. But at least give the game plan a fair try. Use your running backs to soften up the defense. Mix. Keep the opposition off balance. Run when they expect you to throw sometimes and throw when they are set up to stop the run. But do it all within the framework of your coach's game plan. Lean on his wisdom and experience until you have played long enough to develop your own instinct about the quarterback role.

Remember, you may have the greatest arm in the world, plus all the confidence in the world, but *you can't do it all alone!*

Along these lines, it might be good for the beginning quarterback to rely on his ends and backs—and, yes, even his linemen—to help him from time to time in the huddle. Your ends may notice something about the defensive coverage that has escaped you. Listen to them and maybe you can take advantage of a soft spot in the defense. Your linemen may tip you that a defensive tackle on one side is charging very hard on every play. They may feel he can be trapped, so you oblige them by calling a quick trap play. It may

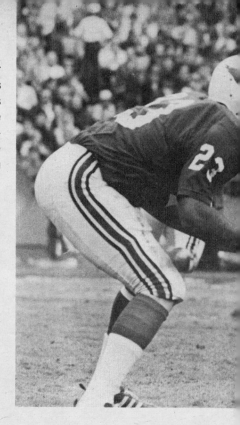

not work, true, but then again it may go for big yardage.

While a quarterback must depend on this kind of information from his teammates, he must also guard against losing control in the huddle. You don't want everyone talking at once, nor can you tolerate six different suggestions on what play to call next. This is a thin line for any quarterback to walk. By all means, encourage your teammates to tip you to things the other club is doing but don't allow it to get out of hand

Cards' Jim Hart (17) has all the qualities of a top pro quarterback.

in the huddle. Let them know you are in charge. Run the huddle with firmness and authority and don't hesitate to tell someone to "Keep quiet."

It is a good idea to confer with your coaches during every time-out and also when the defensive unit is on the field. This is also a good time to ask some of your linemen about what's going on up front. It will make them feel important, as if they are making a key contribution to the game, and will help establish you as leader.

Which brings up another side to quarterbacking. Leadership doesn't just happen. You must work at being a leader, on the field and off the field. You don't have to be popular with everyone on the squad—indeed, this is often impossible—but you do want to command your teammates' respect and confidence. Some of this respect can be built in practice and in the classroom and on the bench. But most of it happens in the pressure of the huddle ... ●

In The Huddle

■ The huddle has long been a symbol of mysticism to football fans, a formation where men meet in secrecy and, conversing in an alien tongue, plot winning strategy. Television has taken followers of professional football into the locker-rooms, onto the bench, into the pre-game briefings, just about everywhere behind the scenes. But the huddle has firmly resisted any such electronic intrusion; it remains inviolate, the last bastion of gridiron intrigue. This has made it all the more maddening for the average fan who would almost certainly sell his soul (or even his season ticket!) for the chance to stick his head into a huddle—just once. For him, life holds no greater frustration.

It doesn't help, either, when the Little Lady pipes up with, "Why do they have to bend over and whisper? Why don't they stand up like men and call their old plays?"

How can she appreciate that the huddle is something special, a sacred temple, as it were, closed to all but a select few, and that decisions of great importance are made there?

Just what *would* you hear if you could eavesdrop on a huddle some Sunday afternoon in Dallas or Denver or Green Bay? Would it be as intriguing and as fascinating as you've imagined all these years in your role as a frustrated outsider? Would you understand the technical language of professional football? Or, might you be disappointed and slightly let down by the whole thing?

Well, "BACKFIELD IN MOTION," is about to give you the chance you've always wanted. That's right—we're going to take you inside a typical pro huddle and, what's more, we'll let you stay in there as the quarterback runs his ball club through a series of offensive downs. You'll hear it like it is, in the language of the pros, and you'll feel the pulse of the game as it unfolds around you. Further, we'll try to put you right inside the quarterback's helmet so you can read his thoughts, experience his doubts, understand his decisions. In a sense, you'll be the quarterback; you'll feel the pressure of leadership and you'll know the deadening weight of responsibility. They call it the "loneliness of command," and that's exactly what it is when

Dallas coach Tom Landry and QB Roger Staubach plot strategy on sideline.

you're the guy calling the plays with the chips smack dab on the line.

And after you leave the huddle, and return to your seat, maybe you will take with you a greater appreciation of the skills required to play quarterback and perhaps you won't be so quick to yell for the quarterback's scalp the next time he blows one on second down and three. Maybe, just maybe, you'll turn to the red-faced critic next to you and say, "Hell, Harry, he couldn't go weak with that motion stuff out of an I-right. Didn't you see the off safety rolling up into the hook zone?" And good old Harry will blink once or twice, shift his cigar to the other side of his big mouth and snort, "What are you, anyway—a quarterback?" You'll just smile and ignore him while you silently contemplate the next play. "Let's see now . . . third and two. That ninety-three pass, with the B back shuffling, ought to work; that is, if he doesn't call it from a sprint left."

As the quarterback prepares for his first offensive series of the game he has several things he wants to achieve right off the bat. The first is that he must establish the superiority of his blockers; he must make the opposition respect the strength and power of his blocking linemen. In the same manner, the baseball pitcher attempts to establish his fastball early in the game, so the batters will be worrying about it later on. Likewise, the wide receiver in pro ball seeks to establish his deep "fly" pattern against the defensive halfback covering him; once he accomplishes this, he has intimidated the defender to a degree, and he can then work his other patterns, knowing that the halfback will be thinking mainly about not being beaten deep. It is important, too, that the quarterback test the effectiveness of his pass blocking, for this will be a crucial factor as the game progresses.

Okay, so it's first down on the offensive team's 20-yard line and you are in the huddle, right in there, leaning over the quarterback's shoulder. And this is what you might hear:

"Okay, men, let's put our hats (helmets) on 'em this first time. I'm gonna give you what you want. Here it is: I-right . . . weak . . . motion . . . Dive thirty-three . . . on two . . . let's get 'em . . . ready—break."

What the quarterback has called on first down is a routine dive play with the No. 3 back, the

Chiefs' Otis Taylor (L) draws pass pattern for quarterback Len Dawson.

fullback, going through the No. 3 hole over right guard. It's a quick-hitting play with a simple handoff and it is called mainly to test the defense and to give the offensive linemen the opportunity to work off their nervous tension by throwing that first block.

As the team breaks the huddle and lines up over the ball, the quarterback checks the defense to see if the Dive-33 play will work. If he feels that the defense is lined up to stop the Dive-33, he will automatic to another play. This is also known as going to an "audible" call, which is nothing more than an alternate play that is given to the rest of the team by a series of number changes at the line of scrimmage. How does the quarterback tip off his teammates that he's going to change the original call? He does it by inserting the snap number (in this case "two") as the start of his signal-calling. So, if he wants to automatic, he starts by barking out, "Set (linemen down in three-point stance) ... Two ... Thirty-nine. Hut-one ... hut-two."

As soon as the rest of the offense hears the number "two" called out, they know the Dive-33 play has been canceled and that the quarterback is about to give them the alternate call, in this case "39"—a quick pitchout to the fullback.

On our first down play, however, the quarterback does not automatic, and so his call sounds like this: "Set ... one ... three ... thirty-nine. Hut-one, hut-two." On the snap number of "two," the line charges, the fullback hits into the No. 3 hole and grinds out three yards up to the 23. It's second down and seven, and you're back in the huddle.

Now the quarterback has to begin an important part of his job—making his teammates believe they can handle the other club, psyching them up, sometimes in subtle tones, other times more directly. "Okay, men, good job. I saw some tough hitting on that one. That's the way to go, Richie; you really popped that tackle." The quarterback doesn't make a speech; nothing like that. He doesn't have the time. He just slips in a few words of praise here, a gentle prod there. Later, some of the linemen might not even remember what he said but, at the time, the words have the desired effect.

"All right, second and seven, fellas. They might be looking for something outside, or maybe a pass. Let's go with I-right ... Power twenty-seven ... on one. Ready—break!"

The play he's called starts with the quarterback sprinting (actually, sprinting in this instance does

Ex-Green Bay QB Bart Starr (15) was one of best third-down play-callers.

not mean running fast) to the right and then making a back handoff to the halfback, the No. 2 back, who veers against the flow into the seven hole. The strategy behind this call on second down is twofold: first, it gives the quarterback a chance to watch the reaction of the defense to the sprint-out action; second, the coaches in the press box upstairs can get an early evaluation of overall defensive coverage.

The snap signal, remember, was "one," so here's how the signals are given at the line of scrimmage: "Set ... two ... ninety-seven. Hut-one!" Note that the "two" is merely a dummy number. If the quarterback had said, "One," it would have indicated an audible call. But there was no audible this time, so the ball is handed back to the halfback who hits the seven hole for a five-yard gain. The ball is on the 28-yard line and it's now third down and two, a crucial point in the first series.

The quarterback keeps working on his team in the huddle. "Great job up front, men. We had to establish that one. Now we're on our way. Let's get 'em."

For the first time in the game, the quarterback is faced with a difficult decision. The percentage strategy might indicate running for the two yards; after all, he got three on the first down and five on second down. "But they'll be in there tight," he says to himself. "They'll stack up the middle looking for the run. My best bet is to give 'em that Power twenty-seven look again, but we'll throw off it instead."

Sticking his head back into the huddle, the quarterback says, "Okay, here it is: Green . . . I-right . . . sprint right . . . ninety-three . . . B shuffle. On three. Ready—break!"

"Green" is the key word in this call. It indicates a forward pass. Whenever the linemen, backs and ends hear "green," they know the ball is going to be put into the air. The offense lines up in the I--formation right and the quarterback sprints to his right after taking the snap. The fullback (No. 3 man) fakes a block and then slips out into the right flat zone to receive a short pass after the quarterback makes the running fake to the halfback. But the defense doesn't go for the inside running fake. The left linebacker drifts out to cover the fullback and he knocks down the pass. The "ninety-three, B shuffle" call fails and

the offense must punt the ball away on fourth down.

But the opening series has at least given the quarterback the "feel" of the game. While the defense is on the field, he has time to talk the situation over with his head coach, and also with the assistant coaches who are spotting

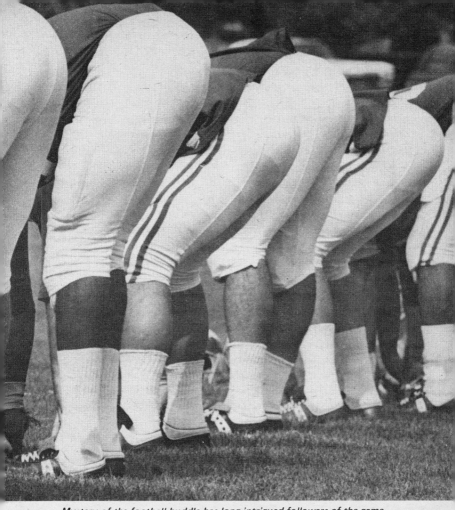

Mystery of the football huddle has long intrigued followers of the game.

the game from upstairs. The quarterback tells his coach, "It looks like they're gonna pinch off the middle on running downs but maybe give us the seven hole." The coach nods in agreement and adds, "And, I don't think they'll show us their short-yardage defense on third and two or three; they may not go into it unless it's third and one." The quarterback makes a mental note of this bit of intelligence. If the opposition is going to save its short-yardage defense (usually a gap defense) for one-yard situations—well, maybe he can take advantage of this later on in the game. From the coaches in the press box he gets some preliminary ideas of how the defense lines up versus the I-right weak motion series. One assistant may even point out the differences in the coverage of the I-right formation on second and seven as compared with third and two. The quarterback assimilates this information and asks himself, "Does this give me any advantages right now?"

Before the offense takes the field again, the quarterback also tries to talk with as many of his players as he can. "New series coming up, fellas. We're ready now, right?" To another group he might say, "Don't get down. We just wanted to try a few things on that first series. We've got the feel now. We can do it next time out."

After an exchange of punts, the offense starts again from its own 32-yard line. The quarterback decides to check the middle linebacker's reaction, so he calls "I-left . . . strong . . . double dive twenty-three . . . on one. Ready—break!" There's no motion (or peel) on this play and the gap is on the tight end side. The play starts with a fake handoff to the fullback going right and then the quarterback continues his pivot and gives to the halfback going over the right guard hole. The initial fake to the fullback is designed to pin down the middle

linebacker and to give the offense an idea of what key he is playing. As the team breaks the huddle, the quarterback turns to his fullback and says, "Remember now, get up there close. This has got to be fast." The fullback gets close but the play is stopped for only a two-yard gain and now it is second and eight on the 34.

Another crisis for the quarterback. The line isn't doing the job on running plays. He's got to prod his linemen a little and yet he doesn't want to make it too strong. It's still early in the game. So, as the team huddles, he looks around and says, "We can move the ball, fellas, but we're going to need better hitting up there. I know you can handle 'em. Plenty of time left."

As he straightens up in the huddle to look across at the defense, the quarterback ponders the situation. "I've run four plays from the I-formation. Now I have to show 'em the Red formation for the first time. Gotta show 'em the passing formation, but I don't want to throw. Okay, I'll try an end run." He bends over and says to the team, "We gotta establish our end run sometime, so let's do it now. We need this one, men. Okay, here it is: Red right . . . Power 29 . . . on two. Ready—break!"

The quarterback surveys the

defense again as he takes his place behind the center. He must look for a number of things. "Are they playing us for run or pass? Check those linebackers. Are they playing loose? How about the cornerbacks—are they ready for bump-and-run coverage? We're showing 'em a passing formation but are they going to honor it . . . or are they playing for the run?"

The defense plays for the end run and stops it for a loss of one yard. Third down and nine on the 33. And now there is no question—the quarterback must put the ball in the air. He has run out of ground play options. The trouble is, the defense knows this too, so the pressure mounts. A football game swings on the success (or failure of third down plays; the quarterback who converts most often in this crucial situation is usually the winning quarterback. It was more than coincidence that Bart Starr was the best third-down quarterback in the NFL during the years that the Green Bay Packers were winning all those championships.

There's no doubt in the quarterback's mind that the defense will be blowing in there on the next play, trying to push him into even deeper trouble. It's a situation that almost invites an all-out rush or a heavy linebacker blitz. The defense can afford to gamble.

The quarterback knows this, and he decides to take advantage of the inevitable defensive rush. "I'll call a screen pass," he says to himself, "and make 'em think twice about blitzing later in the game. I gotta make 'em respect our screens and draws, and there's no better time than right now."

The quarterback feels the pressure at this critical moment. The defense is trying to out-guess and out-maneuver him and, in the huddle, his team is waiting for him to come up with the right call. He suddenly feels very alone and very responsible. But this is the price of leadership. This is why he gets paid so much money. His allotted 25 seconds are running out so he has to hurry now with his decision. "We wanna make it look like a regular pass," he snaps, "so you linemen stay with those blocks. You backs step up in there like you're gonna pass block. Make it look good; we need a big one here. All right, Green . . . red right . . . screen right to fullback . . . on two. And, remember, fellas—stay in there. Ready—break!"

The screen pass call catches the defense by surprise. The fullback takes a short lob pass over the heads of the onrushing defense linemen and gains 11 yards before a cornerback recovers and brings him down. It's first down on the

It's hard for QB to throw well when he's under a heavy pass rush.

44, and everyone feels a lot better.

As the huddle forms, the quarterback resumes his psyching. "Way to go," he exudes. "You guys pulled it off perfectly. Great play, men, great execution."

And then the guessing game starts all over again. To himself, the quarterback reasons, "We just hit 'em with an eleven-yard play. That stung 'em a little, so maybe they'll come back with a stunt this time, maybe a safety blitz or something. If the linebackers are gonna dog (red-dog or blitz), the ends will have 'spy' pass coverage,

and the free safety will be tied up as a tackler. If those ends aren't rushing, maybe I can go with the Power twenty-seven again; I got five yards with it earlier. That's it—I'll run it at 'em again and hope to catch them in a stunt."

In the huddle, he says, "They're expecting a run, so we'll put it in the air. But first, let's make 'em think it's a run. We'll give 'em some play-action. Here's the call: I-right . . . Green . . . fake Power twenty-seven . . . wing corner . . . On three. Ready— break!"

The quarterback has called the

sprint-out play that worked earlier but this time he fakes the back handoff to the halfback and instead throws a quick pass to the wing-back, who runs a corner route near the sideline. The idea here is to catch the opposition moving up to stop what looks like a routine Power 27 run, and then throw the ball on top (or over) the defense. As signals are called, the quarterback checks to see where the free safety is; this is the one man who might stop the play. "Set . . . two . . . nineteen. Hut-one, hut-two, hut-three." The deception works. The defense is suckered into thinking the play is a run. The wingback, meanwhile, runs his corner route and gets open down the field. He looks like he might go all the way but the pass is wobbly and a bit short, and the defense recovers in time to hold it to a 22-yard gain.

The reason the quarterback threw poorly was because he was under a heavy rush. His blocking didn't hold up long enough. Again, as the team leader, he must handle the situation delicately. He's got to let them know they didn't do the job but, at the same time, he must take some of the blame himself. "Okay, men, that should have been a TD. Sorry about it. But we're on our way. We'll get that blocking down better later on, right?"

Notice how the quarterback blames himself for the under-thrown pass, and tries to build up his team's confidence by pointing out that ". . . we're on our way." And then, mildly, he makes the point that the blocking wasn't perfect but that he's sure it will improve. A subtle dig that is not overlooked by the guys on the line—and yet it's done in such a manner, no one gets hot about it. He must always keep in mind that he is at the controls of a high-strung, explosive human machine that is set on a hair trigger. If he berates his linemen too openly, he might lose them for the rest of the game. On the other hand, he can't afford to accept breakdowns without bringing it to their attention.

Most of all, the professional quarterback must always guard his own emotions. He has to present an outwardly calm and confident appearance, no matter what doubts and indecisions he may feel inside. His eyes cannot betray uncertainty or hesitancy. The tone of his voice must be strong and confident. He is never off the hot seat, and so he can't permit himself to relax or to let down. He exists in a climate of continual pressure, a pressure felt by no one else on the field or in the stadium—except you, now that you have shared his ordeal in the huddle. ●

Winning Pass Plays

■ Pass completions do not occur by chance. They are plotted, practiced, perfected and, hopefully, executed on game day. Each move has a special and significant meaning. Distance . . . depth . . . speed . . . deception. Mix them all together and you have the basic elements of a pass pattern.

While the theory of pass offense is much too lengthy to consider in its entirety in a book of this size, as a quarterback you should at least be familiar with a few of the fundamental concepts and what they are intended to achieve on the playing field.

First, it must be mentioned that descriptive terminology differs widely from team to team. A pass route known as a "circle" on one ball club may be called a "banana" on another. A "button-hook" is also known as a "turn-in." And so on. Whatever the name, however, most of the pass routes in high school football are similar in design to those used by the professionals. What differs are the defenses. The NFL clubs use basically a 4-3-4 defense while

high schools and colleges employ 6-3-2 or 6-2-3 or 5-3-3 or 5-4-2 alignments. No matter, the pass routes to be discussed in this chapter are always run about the same way. And the aim is always the same: get your man open and hit him with the forward pass!

If you examine some of the basic individual routes in Diagrams A, B, C, D, E, F, G, H, I and J you will see that most patterns consist of "sister" moves—that is, the first few steps in each route (called the "stem" by some coaches) start out identically and then break off in opposite directions or angles depending on the designation of the play called by the quarterback.

In the accompanying diagrams—which, by the way, are drawn for the *right end* position—the Os represent the offensive team and the Vs designate the defensive backs.

To illustrate the workings of these patterns, let's examine Diagram A and Diagram B:

A) SQUARE-OUT: The receiver comes off the line in a

John Brodie of the 49ers is a master at throwing the tough sideline pass.

"stem" that goes anywhere from eight to 12 yards. The depth of this initial penetration into the secondary is dependent on two factors: 1) who the defender is—whether he plays the receiver closely or drops back and plays "off" him, and 2) what the down and yardage situation happens to be. If the distance needed for a first down is eight yards, then the receiver tries to penetrate to at least a depth of nine yards before squaring out toward the sideline. This is to ensure a first down upon reception of the ball. Catching the ball at seven yards would leave him shy of the first down.

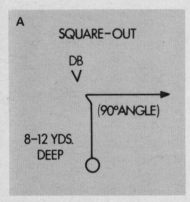

The square-out pattern is usually called when the quarterback—or one of the receivers—finds that a defender is favoring the inside of the receiver's moves—that is, guarding more closely against a break to the inside than against a possible outside move. If the

square-out pattern is successful once or twice, the receiver may find that the defender is now conscious of this outside move, which could set him up for the square-in pattern.

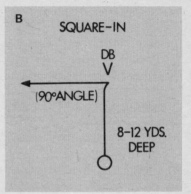

B) SQUARE-IN: As mentioned, this is the "sister" move to the square-out. The route starts the same way with the receiver driving straight off the line and directly at the defender. The variation occurs when the receiver, faking a move similar to his square-out break, cuts instead to the inside. Ideally, this deceptive break catches the defensive man in an instant of indecision and gives the pass-catcher the advantage of a step or two. As with all "sister" patterns, the square-out and the square-in aid and abet one another.

Diagrams C and D, called by most teams down-and-in and down-and-out patterns, are similar "sister" maneuvers. Their "stems" are 12-14 yards, slightly deeper than the square-out and square-in routes, and the angle of break is less acute, 45 degrees as compared to 90 degrees.

Diagrams E and F have "stems" that begin at an angle and the pattern involves two deceptive changes of direction instead of one, as with the other four patterns.

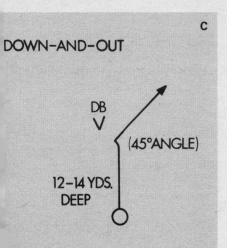

C

DOWN-AND-OUT

DB
V

(45°ANGLE)

12-14 YDS.
DEEP

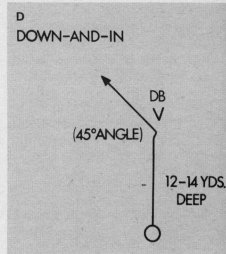

D

DOWN-AND-IN

DB
V

(45°ANGLE)

12-14 YDS.
DEEP

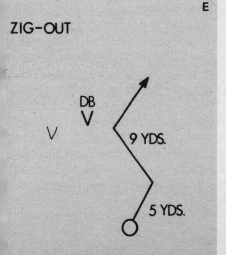

E

ZIG-OUT

DB
V

V

9 YDS.

5 YDS.

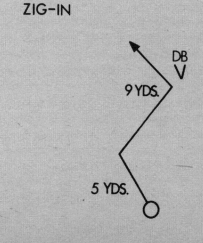

F

ZIG-IN

DB
V

9 YDS.

5 YDS.

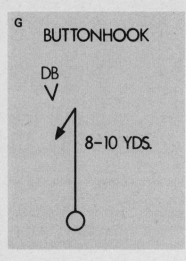

G

BUTTONHOOK

DB
V

8–10 YDS.

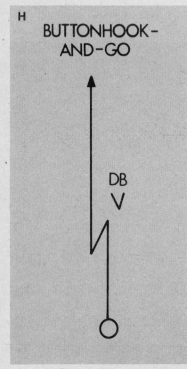

H

BUTTONHOOK-
AND-GO

DB
V

The buttonhook route shown in Diagram G requires the end to drive straight down on the defensive back, forcing him to retreat a few steps, and then make a quick turn (or buttonhook) back toward the quarterback. This is an extremely difficult pass to cover, and so it becomes a good percentage pass for you to throw. Diagram H traces a "sister" move which is known as the buttonhook-and-go. This is used when the defensive man starts rushing up tight to stop the buttonhook pattern; the receiver fakes the buttonhook turn and then races down the field into a deeper receiving area. The defensive man, caught coming in, usually has trouble changing direction to pick up the receiver.

The quick slant-in and the slant-out shown in Diagrams I and J are just what the names imply— quick, slashing routes which require a short, hard toss by the quarterback. They are effective and they also minimize the chance of interception since the ball is in the air for just a second or two.

Thus far this discussion has centered on the offensive right end position. Of course, the same routes can be run by the wide receiver on the other side or by the tight end. In Diagrams K and L are depicted two basic routes run by backfield men, the circle

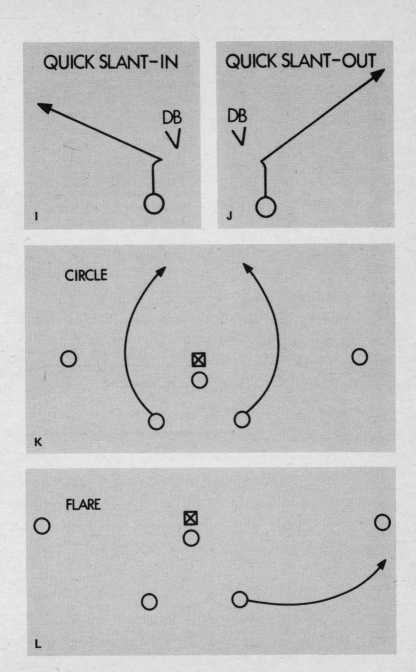

QUICK SLANT-IN

DB

I

QUICK SLANT-OUT

DB

J

CIRCLE

K

FLARE

L

pass and the flare pass. The latter is sometimes known as a "safety valve" because the quarterback can dump the ball to his flare man in the event his downfield receivers are covered or when the defense breaks through and doesn't give him the time he needs to wait for a deep pattern to develop.

All of these moves are individual routes. When combined with other individual routes, they become a complete pattern.

Let's see how individual routes are incorporated into a general pass pattern by considering the right end square-out play shown in Diagram No. 1. This is a three-man pattern. The split end on the left runs a deep down-and-in route to draw the defensive safetyman out of the way. The flanker back on the right side runs what is called a "fly" route, racing along the sideline to lure the defensive cornerback away from the intended target zone. The right end (sometimes known as the tight end) drives straight at his man and then cuts sharply to the outside, using the square-out maneuver described earlier in this chapter. He runs what is known as an "underneath" route— that is, he breaks for the sideline right after the flanker has gone by him on his fly route.

A heads-up quarterback must always be aware of his entire pattern. It's important to know what each of your receivers is doing

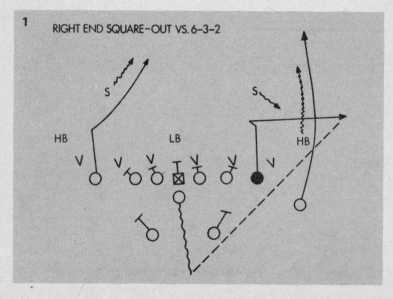

1 RIGHT END SQUARE-OUT VS. 6-3-2

because their movements influence the defensive secondary and this, in turn, can affect the direction, distance and timing of your pass.

Diagram No. 2 outlines a sequence pattern that may be employed after the right end square-out (No. 1) has been successful. Everything is the same—except that the end adds another move this time. He runs his normal square-out but then, as the defender closes in on him, he turns sharply up the sideline and runs into a deeper receiving zone.

This is where a receiver can pass along helpful information to the quarterback. If the end senses that the defender is being intimidated by the regular square-out

play, he can suggest the square-out and up pattern to the quarterback, who may not be aware of how the defensive man is covering the receiver. It is to your advantage as the quarterback to keep these lines of communication open with your receiver. In fact, it doesn't hurt to turn to one of your ends and ask, "How tight is that guy playing you? Think you can beat him with a buttonhook?"

In Diagram No. 3 we see the buttonhook route as part of a three-man pattern against a 6-2-3 defense. The wide receivers on both sides run deep routes in an effort to clear out the middle zone. The right end, meanwhile, bolts off the line of scrimmage

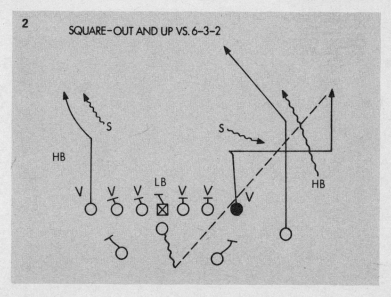

2   SQUARE-OUT AND UP VS. 6-3-2

and drives down on the opposing safetyman, hoping to make him retreat a few steps. As soon as he sees the safety back-pedaling, the receiver pulls up sharply and hooks back toward the line of scrimmage. This screens the defender from the ball and gives the quarterback a good stationary target.

The screen pass is not one of the easiest passes to set up or to throw. It requires precision timing and coordination among all 11 men on offense. It is presented here merely to give the young quarterback a visual idea of what the play looks like in the playbook. (Diagram No. 4).

The idea, of course, is to bait the defense into a strong pass rush. As soon as the defensive rush carries across the line of scrimmage, the offensive center, right guard and right tackle slide out into the flat to form a three-man screen. The fullback pretends to pass block for the count of two, and then he drifts out into the flat behind the screen. The quarterback makes a preliminary pass drop of several yards and then, as if under pressure by the defensive rush, drops back even farther. Just before the pass rushers get to him, the quarterback lobs a soft pass over their heads to the fullback, who is waiting out behind the screen.

To be effective, the screen pass requires some good "acting" by the quarterback, whose job it is to

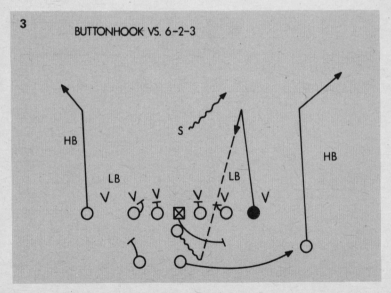

3

BUTTONHOOK VS. 6-2-3

make the defense believe he is in serious trouble. Fran Tarkenton of Minnesota is a master at this dramatic touch, as are Roman Gabriel of Los Angeles, John Brodie of San Francisco and Len Dawson of Kansas City. Note that all are experienced veterans who have had many years to learn the nuances of the age-old screen pass.

To summarize, there are a number of key points for young quarterbacks to concentrate on:

1. Know the individual abilities and habits of your receivers.

2. Work on single pass routes before worrying about the overall pattern plays.

3. If you are playing sandlot or high school ball, use one and two-man patterns instead of four-man patterns that strip you of much-needed blocking.

4. Make certain that your receiver always gets enough depth on third down to assure a first down if he catches the ball.

5. Seek valuable information from your receivers in the huddle or during timeouts.

6. Have a mental picture of what every man in the pass pattern is doing at all times, even though your concentration is focused on your primary receiver.

7. Use short, quick passes whenever possible to reduce the chance of a costly interception.

8. Finally, remember that pass patterns do not just happen. They are the result of practice, timing and teamwork. ●

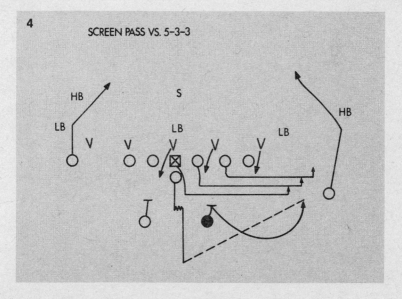

4   SCREEN PASS VS. 5-3-3

Scouting the Pros

■ Would-be quarterbacks of the present generation have unlimited opportunities to learn by observation. Pro football expansion has brought NFL-style play into most of the nation's major cities. Ever-widening television coverage, with its excellent stop-action and slow motion re-plays, provides a virtual classroom-at-home for any youngster who is serious about studying the great quarterbacks at work.

There is much to be gained by watching the pro quarterbacks: the lightning release of Joe Namath, the quick set-up of Len Dawson, the guile of Fran Tarkenton, the classic throwing motion of Roman Gabriel, the scrambling of Roger Staubach, the coolness under pressure of Sonny Jurgensen. Each professional, in his own way, has something to offer the young quarterback who takes the time to study and observe.

Next time you go to a pro game (or, for that matter, a college game) or watch two NFL teams on television, make a mental check-list of the quarterback techniques you want to look for. Naturally, you won't be able to see everything; things happen too fast. But you can absorb many of the mechanics if you keep your eyes riveted to the quarterback and resist the temptation to follow the ball.

Start right at the beginning and notice how John Brodie of the San Francisco 49ers positions himself behind the center with his hands firmly placed to receive the ball, his back fairly straight and his head up so he can scan the defensive team across from him. Brodie, one of the game's premier passers and the league's MVP in 1971, is not particularly fast but watch how quickly he pushes away from the center and gets back to his passing depth. This one movement alone saves Brodie a precious second that he can use while he's waiting to release the ball. It should be mentioned too that John could not always set up this fast and that in the beginning he had trouble with his pass drop. But constant work and practice finally made him one of the best in the business.

Most professional scouts and talent men agree that Joe Namath of the New York Jets combines all the attributes of the ideal quarter-

Roger Staubach of Dallas is a leader of new generation of NFL quarterbacks.

back. They give him perfect ratings in the following three categories: reaction under pressure, set-up speed and throwing, and he is accorded almost perfect marks for leadership and ability to read defenses.

Earlier in this book, the matter of confidence was discussed at length. It was pointed out that confidence is an indispensable item in the make-up of a quarterback. Well, Namath typifies this positive attitude. "I always feel I can complete the pass," he explains without bravado. This confidence in his quick release and in the accuracy of his tosses enables Joe to wait a split-second longer before throwing the ball, and it allows him to throw into tough defensive coverage. If you are fortunate enough to see Namath play, make sure you note the Jet star's perfect overhand throwing motion and his full follow-through.

In his younger, healthier days, Johnny Unitas had one of the quickest releases in the NFL, a whip-like snap of arm and wrist that flew the ball off his fingertips. Johnny U.'s passing form, even now, is something to see: ball held firmly to the body on the drop, a pump fake here and there, eyes

Young Dennis Shaw of Buffalo (16) has great arm, needs more experience.

78

always focused on the play in front of him, a classic overhand arm delivery and the pro follow-through, arm extended after the ball, wrist turned in, fingers firm. This is the way the book says a football should be thrown.

The only quarterback in the NFL who approaches Namath in overall quarterback form is the veteran Sonny Jurgensen of the Washington Redskins. But in Jurgensen you will see a variance in passing style. Whereas Namath and Brodie and Unitas throw straight overhand, bringing the ball high past the right ear, Sonny often makes his delivery with a quick sidearm motion—well, maybe not completely sidearm but close to it.

Jurgensen's release is faster than any except Namath. He has a rubbery, slingshot arm that can hit a receiver right on the numbers 40 yards down the field.

If you want an example of a standard pocket passer, Norm Snead of the Giants might be the man to study. Snead is a big fellow, 6-4 and 220, and he has a powerful throwing arm. His pass drop and release are slightly slower than some other quarterbacks but he offsets this with great strength. He often releases the ball with tacklers hanging all over him. With his extra height he is able to see clearly all over the field, and so he completes many passes that a shorter quarterback might not be able to hit—just because he was screened off by the onrushing defense and couldn't see his receiver get open.

While Len Dawson doesn't have a great throwing arm or a quick release, the veteran Kansas City Chiefs' quarterback is a master at working a game. That is, Len controls the tempo of the game with brilliant play selection and clever ball-handling. He knows how to use his runners to set the defense up for a counter play or for a pass. His end-around calls to Frank Pitts in Super Bowl IV against the Minnesota Vikings were classics of timing and deception. Dawson usually manages to finish among the NFL's top passers because his brilliance as a field manager makes the rival defense highly vulnerable to the aerial strike.

Speaking of rivals, they hate to play against Dawson. Said one NFL defensive tackle, "Len always keeps you off balance, always guessing. You never know what to expect."

Dawson's great experience, of course, has made him a keen student of quarterback strategy. He

Len Dawson (16) of Chiefs is a master at play selection and strategy.

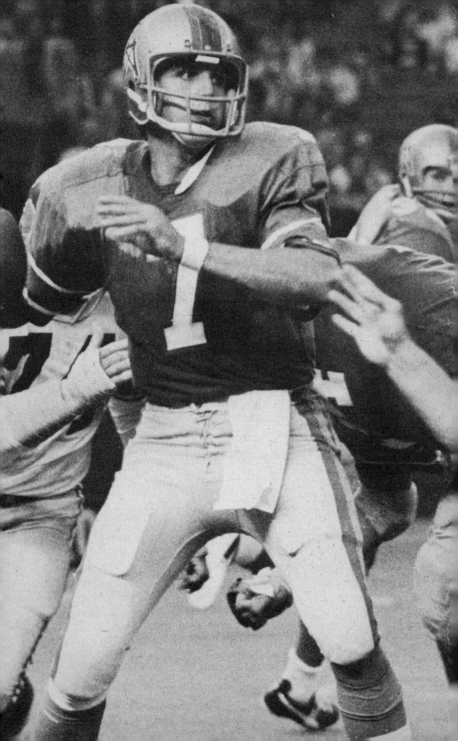

has proved that there are more ways to win a football game than by passing alone. This should be a good lesson for any young quarterback. Learn to use all your personnel, all your plays—and don't rely on just your arm.

Bart Starr, the heady veteran who led the Green Bay Packers to their memorable Super Bowl victories, was a quarterback much like Dawson. He worked his game plan like a master, probing the defense, seeking a weakness and then exploiting it. Starr was an example of a quarterback who made it big in the NFL despite having only a fair passing arm.

Fran Tarkenton of the Minnesota Vikings doesn't have a lot of things—size, speed or a strong arm—and yet Fran can find a hundred different ways to win out there on the field. First, he is a very intelligent quarterback who knows his opponents perhaps better than they know themselves (again, a reminder of how valuable study is to the young quarterback). Second, Fran is always a threat to run with the ball, or to scramble. This gives defensive linemen fits of rage and frustration. It also keeps them "honest." They have to stay alert for one of Fran's scrambles.

Scrambling is not advised for

Patriots' Jim Plunkett (16) may have best arm of all young NFL QBs.

young quarterbacks, at least not as an important part of your technique. As with a fake, use the scramble from time to time to get out of trouble or to make a broken play go for yardage. But don't depend on the scramble as a winning maneuver all the time.

"I only scramble when I have to," explains Tarkenton, maybe the most famous scrambler of

Great things are expected of Houston's young Dan Pastorini, a coming star.

them all. "I never start a play with the intention of running with the ball. That only happens when I am forced out of the pocket. Someone once asked me if I practiced the scramble play. That's silly. A scramble is an improvization; it happens but it isn't planned."

Among the younger quarterbacks in the NFL, Roger Staubach of Dallas, the MVP in 1971, is also noted for his scrambles but, like Tarkenton, Roger plays them down. He'd rather concentrate on his basic quarterback form, he says, and not think about running all over the gridiron.

Staubach's strongest assets are his leadership ability (he's an Annapolis graduate who served four years in the U.S. Navy) and his reaction to pressure situations. Dallas coach Tom Landry says Roger is improving at reading defenses but that he needs more experience in this area, which harkens back to something Y.A. Tittle wrote in the introduction to this book: "There is a great deal to learn about playing this game, no matter what position you play. It takes time."

Bob Griese of the Miami Dolphins, who was Staubach's foe in Super Bowl VI, is a good example of a disciplined quarterback. Bob follows coach Don Shula's game plan right down to the last letter. He has faith in the Dolphin runners, Jim Kiick and Larry Csonka, and he gets the most out of their talents. By mixing his running game with the passing attack, Bob can generate a real ball-control offense. This is the way Starr did it for many years at Green Bay with Jim Taylor and Paul Hornung.

Attention here has been focused mainly on the more experienced quarterbacks in the NFL. But there are some brilliant young fellows to try to emulate too. Perhaps the most promising passer of all is big Jim Plunkett of the New England Patriots. He has a great arm and exceptional poise for a youngster in the pro ranks.

Also in or near Plunkett's class are Terry Bradshaw of the Pittsburgh Steelers, Dennis Shaw of the Buffalo Bills and Archie Manning of the New Orleans Saints. Any or all of them are worth watching if you want to pick up valuable hints on how to play quarterback.

But remember this: each of these quarterbacks started from the beginning, just as you are, and it took time and practice and desire to make it to the NFL. You can learn much by watching them, the Namaths, the Dawsons, the Staubachs, but you must supply the dedication and drive yourself. ●

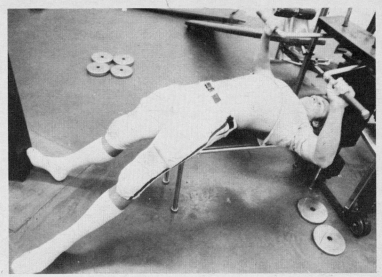
A smart player works the year round to keep himself in top condition.

QB: A Job For All Seasons

■ Football may be a builder of character and a maker of men but don't expect the game to work any miracles for you unless you give it your best effort. It's the old formula of output equaling input.

Whether you play quarterback or defensive tackle, your responsibility as a player does not end with the final whistle. It continues into your daily life and it affects many of the things you do at home, at work and in school.

Actually, the average sandlot or high school player spends less than five hours on the playing field in games each season. This is based on an average eight-game season, which breaks down to a total of 480 minutes. Divide this in half (since most players go only one way in today's two-platoon system) and you get 240 minutes of actual playing time per man. Of course, practice time greatly increases this total but the fact remains that, out of the entire

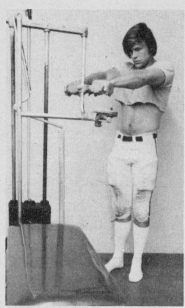

Sound weight program can help young quarterback strengthen forearms.

Any kind of cycling activity, even this machine, is good for legs.

year, the typical football player is plying his trade for a very short period of time.

The smart player, however, does not measure his season in minutes; he sees it as a year-round proposition. If he is truly dedicated, he uses the lessons learned in football to guide him through his everyday life. On the practice field he has learned to work hard and to accept discipline and supervision, so he tries to apply this training to his school, to his job or at home.

If you are serious about a career in football, you will be asked to pay a price in the off-

season just as you do during the season. You must attempt to keep your mind oriented by "thinking football" and your body in good condition by some kind of a training program.

A sound training program—even one that you plan for yourself without the help of coaches—is based on two factors: 1) a sensible diet and 2) plenty of physical conditioning work.

It may be that your coach will advise you to try and put on some weight between seasons, especially if you are a defensive lineman. But eating a lot of fattening foods is not the way to achieve a desired weight increase. You should eat regularly, eat only good food and make sure you combine your diet with daily workouts. Now, an off-season workout doesn't have to be as long or as strenuous as what you do during football practice in the fall. You needn't bother with calisthenics, unless it's just to loosen up. The main thing is to do lots of running. This is the best way to keep your entire body in trim—legs, stomach, wind. Running is the best physical conditioner of them all.

There are different kinds of running you can do. You can do some distance work and then short sprints to improve your start and your quickness. You don't have to run hard every day but you should put yourself on some kind of a regular schedule and then stay with it. This is where the football-learned discipline will come to your aid.

Football is a specialized sport and it requires specific use of certain muscles. If, for example, you are a defensive back you might want to practice running backwards during your workouts. This is what you are required to do when you cover a receiver in a game, so why not work to improve this specific skill? Similarly, offensive backs can start their practice sprints from the backfield stance they use in games.

Lifting weights can be useful in many cases but only when you are given a specific program by someone experienced in this field. Lifting weights just for the sake of lifting is of no value and might, in fact, hamper you as a football player. Before you go on a weight program, check with your coach and take his advice. He probably can tell you how much to lift, how often to work with the weights and so on.

Often, the best exercise is not a carefully planned program of calisthenics and weightlifting but rather doing those things that are a normal part of a young fellow's life—swimming, bicycle riding, basketball, baseball, skating.

The main thing is to keep your mind and your body busy when you are not playing football. Remember, it is easier to maintain good condition than to achieve it.

It may sound corny and trite—but sleep is also essential to good body-building. Don't cheat yourself of the rest that will give you muscle tone and stamina. The old saying about not being able to burn the candle at both ends applies doubly if you hope to maintain the mental and physical condition needed to play football.

Since this book is directed primarily to younger players, it might be a good idea to mention something about school. If you are trying out for junior high or high school teams—or even college—you've got to stay eligible. Most schools today demand a certain level of scholastic achievement by every student. This means that if you fail in class—well, you won't be playing football or anything else, at least until you get your grades up where they belong.

Don't fall into the trap of relaxing in your studies just because the football season is over. Discipline yourself to study hard and get good grades. This, after all, is more important to you than football or any other game. Keep things in their proper perspective.

Some truly great football players have been unable to go on to college ball or to the NFL from high school because they goofed off in class. They thought their football ability would carry them through, but it didn't. So hit those books, just like you hit the line.

Playing football is fine but never lose sight of the fact that it is only a means to an end. You can't play football all your life. Someday the game will be behind you and it's then that you will need the education to make a place for yourself in society.

In the meantime, though, you are the quarterback... ●

It's important to loosen up major muscles before every practice.

Don't give up daily exercises just because football season ends.

The Ball Carrier

■ There is, in the modern running back, a blend of qualities that makes him easily the most versatile and dangerous offensive player in the history of the sport. He is runner, receiver, blocker, passer and sometimes kicker. He is a one-man arsenal, a scoring time bomb with a short fuse, a game-breaker in every sense of the word.

Halfbacks and fullbacks have lost their traditional identities in the fast-changing modern game. At one time, the typical fullback was big, slow, strictly a power runner; the halfback was a smaller, quicker man. It was easy to tell them apart in a crowded room. But no longer is this true. To survive the demands of today's game, a running back must possess both size and swiftness. One of these is seldom enough (although Mike Garrett of San Diego and Mercury Morris of Miami, little men who get by on blazing speed and balance, are notable exceptions to the rule).

Actually, the present-day running back has been shaped by his environment, by the rapid evolution of a new breed of defensive specialist—big, mobile men with a wide range of pursuit. Hurryin' Hugh McElhenny, one of the NFL's greatest running backs with the San Francisco 49ers in the 1950s, a man they reverently called "The King," shakes his head when he watches today's defenders at work. "I don't think I could have gotten across the line of scrimmage if I were playing now," he says. "These tackles are faster than some of the safetymen who played a few years ago. It takes a helluva back to run the football today."

Indeed it does. It takes a back who goes 220 or better and who can turn the hundred yards in 10 seconds or less. It takes a runner with power and deception. It takes a man who can bulldoze his way through a pack of 260-pound linesmen, shake off a tenacious linebacker with arms like a blacksmith and then accelerate past a lithe defensive back with 9.6 speed. It takes a gifted athlete with sure hands in the open field and a trigger-fast brain in the clutches. It takes a tough, durable pro, capable of performing week after week under the punishing blows of anti-social defensive mastodons.

Jimmy Brown, the legendary Cleveland Browns' runner, was such a

Gale Sayers (40), ex-Bear star, had natural instincts of a great runner.

ball-carrier, an iron man who successfully withstood the test of time and defense. So is his successor at Cleveland, Leroy Kelly, ex-NFL rushing champion. Gale Sayers, late of the Bears, combined speed, a dazzling change of pace and keen instinct to perform miracles in the open field, although a series of crippling knee injuries forced him to retire. Ken Willard of San Francisco has the power to bowl over a defensive end and the speed to out-run a corner back. Cut from the same mold are Calvin Hill of the Cowboys, Ron Johnson of the Giants, Larry Csonka of the Dolphins, Larry Brown of the Redskins, John Brockington of the Packers, John Riggins of the Jets, O.J. Simpson of the Bills, Dave Osborn of the Vikings, Willie Ellison of the Rams, Denver's Floyd Little and Detroit's Mel Farr.

Greatness in a runner is also measured in poise and confidence and the intuitive ability to make the big play under intense pressure. It is said, too, that being a running back is a state of mind, a sense of being someone special, an aristocrat in a ruffian's game. Whatever, the running back, the man with the football, lends an extraordinary excitement to professional sports. ●

Get Those Extra Yards

■ The men who carry the football are linked to a common cause, almost as old as the game itself: advance the ball at any cost. Run into them, over them, through them or around them. 'But advance the ball!

This sums up the main responsibility of a running back in a few words. But behind the advance-at-any-cost creed there must be a special kind of desire. Now this is true with all positions in the game of football, but perhaps it is just a little bit truer about the running back. Maybe it is because the price he pays is higher. Maybe it is because the rewards are rarely equal to the punishment. Whatever the reason, desire must be listed as the No. 1 priority.

There is absolutely no substitute for this basic ingredient. In the history of football, many different types of runners have risen to greatness—small men, big men, slow men, fast men—but never has one achieved this pinnacle without possessing a burning desire to win. If you look at the best teams in college or professional ball you will find they are successful because they win so many games in the fourth quarter, indeed in the last few minutes. This is where desire comes in, when the body aches and the mind is weary and the heart grows faint from total effort. This is when the players with desire draw on that hidden reserve of strength and overcome their rivals.

If you are serious about becoming a running back, you must start by always thinking in terms of winning football games. Players who want to win—who tell themselves that winning is their goal—stand a good chance of doing just that.

This is not to say that winning in football is the only thing that matters in life. Football, after all, is still only a game, not a life-and-death affair, and defeat does not mean the end. The point here is that the winning attitude you develop as a running back (or as a player at any other position) will be useful to you in whatever

Mel Farr (24) of Lions says all running backs know "... a little fear."

direction your later life takes. Football is an excellent training ground for the battles you will have to fight in adulthood.

When sizing up the offensive backfield candidates, most coaches will look for desire first and aggressiveness second. Aggressiveness is an asset that can be developed in an athlete, although naturally it is more prevalent in some than in others.

Usually, a boy's degree of aggressiveness will be revealed in his first contact practice or scrimmage session. First impressions, they say, are lasting—so it's important that you be prepared to give everything you've got when your turn comes to carry the ball. In most cases, sandlot and high school coaches have huge squads to trim down and very little time in which to do it. This means they must make quick decisions on the potential of the boys trying out for the team. A coach has to get his roster cut to a workable size so he can organize practice schedules and get necessary work done. Under this tight timetable, he cannot afford the luxury of considering a boy who does not show at least some sign of desire and aggressiveness. Maybe these ingredients are present inside but the coach does not have the time to discover them.

So, it's up to you—from that very first day! Keep this in mind.

Even desire and aggressiveness will be of little use if you do not show up in top physical condition. It is necessary for many athletes to punish themselves to achieve this condition. Those who are willing to pay the price will soon find that they are rapidly moving past boys of equal ability who prefer to take the easy road.

This is something the experienced coach will detect, too. The athletes who work harder and push themselves that little bit extra will rise to the top, like cream. Remember, on the lower levels of the game—in junior high and in high school—there is no stationary period in football. Either a player improves every day, or he deteriorates. If you strive to improve yourself as little as one percent during daily practice, you'll find that toward the end of the season you will be quite capable of performing the tasks that are required of you.

Physical condition is vital to you as a running back. Perhaps no other position on the team requires as much stamina, speed and durability. If you doubt this, take a look at the average length of careers of professional running backs. Players like Ron Johnson of the Giants, Larry Csonka of the Miami Dolphins, Steve Owens of Detroit and Larry Brown of Wash-

Even durable backs like Miami's Larry Csonka (39) face injury risk.

ington—to mention four of the brilliant young runners in the NFL—quite likely will have much shorter careers than, say, some defensive linesmen, centers or linebackers of the same age. The fatality rate among running backs is the highest of any position—and with good reason! The ball-carrier takes constant, body-pounding punishment. He is double-teamed high and low by tacklers; he is blind-sided at the knees. He is gang-tackled and mauled by huge defensive specialists. When he isn't carrying the ball, he is hurling himself into opposing linebackers as a blocker, or racing down the field to wipe out a half-back.

Most running backs, as you will learn, accept this pounding as part of the job. The excitement and exhilaration of the position help them overcome the ever-present fear of being injured.

But the fear is there just the same. Mel Farr, the Detroit Lions' fine runner, puts it this way:

"The running back always has a little fear in him. You know you've got that ball, and wherever the ball is, that's where the crowd is going to be. And getting tackled is a thing that hurts. You know, nobody in his right mind wants to go ramming head-on into someone else. But when you get out on that football field, I think you tend to forget all this. And then that little fear just makes you run faster and try harder."

Pittsburgh Steeler linebacker

Andy Russell has another view on the subject of fear:

"The fear of football players is not the fear of pain, but rather the fear that an injury will keep them from doing their job. In this business you can be dedicated, work hard, prepare yourself physically and mentally and in most fields you would succeed because of your attitude. In football, all that can be wiped out in one second and, no matter what your attitude is, you just can't do your job."

The point here is that you have a better chance of avoiding injury as a running back if you keep yourself in sound physical shape. Injury is always a possibility, of course, but if you run fast and hit hard and keep your eyes open, the odds are more *with* you than against you. Players get hurt more often when they are going half-speed or loafing.

Although there is a good deal of individuality to the running back position, the beginner must also think unselfishly in terms of teamwork. This is something many youngsters forget: teamwork, a cohesive effort among 11 players, is the essence of football.

If you do not place team success above your personal desires, then you are of no use to your coach. The outcome of a close game often depends on team uni-ty. There is no place for an individual player who goes his own way. If, for instance, the quarterback calls on your running mate to carry the ball on a try for the winning touchdown, you must block or carry out your assigned fake just as hard and just as aggressively as if *you* were the ball-carrier. This is team unity, every man doing his job to the best of his ability, not for the glory but rather in the interest of winning for his team.

Size is a more flexible item among ball-carriers than among defensive linemen, who should be big and strong. Most coaches would prefer a big, fast running back, of course. However, if you are small, you can make up for a lack of height and weight by quickness and hustle and desire. Some of the game's greatest runners, men like Mike Garrett of San Diego, are midgets compared to their running mates but play like giants because of their desire to excel.

There is a place for you as a running back in football if you measure up to the basic requirements. Let's review them once again before moving on to the more specific aspects of this position:

Desire ... aggressiveness ... good physical condition ... and a dedicated, unselfish attitude. ●

Fundamental blocking is what opened this hole for Raiders' Pete Banaszak.

Fundamentals Come First

■ The word "fundamentals" keeps cropping up again and again in any discussion of football, as does the term "basics." But no matter how many times they are repeated, they aren't enough. Strip the game of its flashy formations, sensational pass plays, sleight-of-hand deception and you'll find that nothing really works unless it is based on fundamentals, solid, plain old everyday fundamentals. Run. Block. Tackle. Pursue. Hit and be hit. Nothing fancy here, just basic.

A running back is no different from any other player when it comes to learning the fundamentals of his position, and practicing until he can do them in his sleep. There is no other way to become a *good* ball-carrier. It takes study, hard work on the field, mental application and patience.

You may have exceptional speed, good size and a flair for

running the ball and yet you'll never be the best if you ignore the groundwork of your position. Such items as stance, start, taking the handoff and making use of your blockers must be worked on until they become second nature to you. You can't expect to break away on that long touchdown run if you line up incorrectly, get off the ball poorly and mess up the exchange with the quarterback.

Even All Pro players in the National Football League, backs like Larry Brown of Washington, Calvin Hill of Dallas, John Brockington of Green Bay, Emerson Boozer of N.Y., and O.J. Simpson of Buffalo, recognize the importance of basic backfield play. They spend part of each practice working on such things as stance, getaway and the timing of the exchange with the quarterback. They may be super-stars in the big league but they take nothing for granted. If it means staying out after practice to polish up one particular area of play, they do it—because they know that success depends on how well versed they are in the basics.

If the professionals, the top men in their field, consider the fundamentals this important, imagine how important they are to you as a beginner. Once you accept this concept you should be in the right frame of mind to

Most backs start from 3-point sprinter's stance, shown from front.

move on to the more specific aspects of running the football.

STANCE

There are two stances preferred by most coaches, the three-point (or sprinter's) stance and the semi-upright stance. Which one you use will be determined, no doubt, by which your coach feels is the best for you, and also which one he believes is the superior stance.

Inside (or near) hand is underneath as back gets set to take handoff.

Running back should "look" the ball into his hands on every exchange.

Let's consider the three-point stance first, since this seems to be the most widely accepted of the two:

Take a sprinter's stance, spreading the feet up to about eight inches apart. The toe of your back foot (and it can be either left or right depending on your position and the formation you are running from) is even with the heel of your forward foot. If your right leg is back, then your right hand touches the ground as the third of your three "points." The other arm rests in a relaxed fashion across the thigh of the opposite leg. There must be weight placed on the supporting hand (the hand touching the ground) to give you maximum speed straight ahead when you move off the mark. Placing the weight on this supporting hand reduces lateral mobility but lateral movement is secondary at this stage. You must go forward.

Keep your shoulders square, tail high, head up and eyes looking straight ahead. The "up" arm, the one resting across your thigh, should have the fist clenched.

From this stance you should be able to move quickly and effortlessly off the mark when the ball is snapped.

The semi-upright stance is exactly what the name implies. You stand up instead of crouching in the sprinter's position with your legs spread about shoulder width, toes turned in slightly, and your hands gripping your legs just above the knee. As with the three-point stance, the head is held high and the eyes are forward. The weight in this stance is primarily on the balls of the feet. The advantage of this semi-upright stance is that it enables the back to make quick starts laterally as well as straight ahead. Most coaches seem to believe that the three-point stance offers the best body balance, and also that it permits a quicker getaway with less wasted motion. In this position, the body is leaning forward, supported by the hand touching the ground, and is ready to move quickly ahead as soon as the ball is snapped.

There is a natural tendency to raise up slightly as you come off the mark in the three-point

stance. This is okay as long as you avoid coming into a complete stand-up position. By staying low, back and butt parallel to the ground, knees slightly flexed, you can uncoil better and thus hit into the line with more velocity.

Whatever stance you use, work hard to perfect it. You can do this before practice or even in your room at home. Remember, if you line up properly and pay attention to each separate detail of the stance, your chances of running a good play are that much better. On the other hand, if you relax and get sloppy about your stance, you may not be ready to explode off the mark when the ball is snapped.

START

The start is the most important single phase in football. Winning plays are the result of 11 men getting off the ball smoothly and quickly on the same count.

As was pointed out, backfield men can improve their starts by assuming a good stance and then working to make it better. You don't have to be a 10-second man to be a good running back, providing you can cover the first five yards with quickness and body control. Despite the fact that a gridiron is 100 yards long, football is a game played mainly in short, quick bursts. Usually the

Here's another method of taking a handoff—with the inside elbow up.

Front view of same exchange shows how ball can be hidden during exchange.

Redskins' Larry Brown (43) gets good grip on ball after taking handoff.

leading running backs in college and pro ball are those who travel those first five yards in the fastest time.

For the best possible start, *make sure that your first move is forward.* Many inexperienced runners unthinkingly take a small backward step before going ahead; this one instant of hesitation can ruin the timing of the whole play.

You have one big advantage being on the offense: you know the snap count; the defense doesn't. Train yourself to anticipate the count—that is, prepare your body to shoot forward as the snap count nears. Don't "tip" the play by leaning to the front; smart defensive players look for these

giveaways. The trick is to mentally picture yourself firing out as the ball is centered. Get your grey matter working before the snap.

The quarterback's cadence can often help you get this little jump. If, for instance, the snap number is three, the quarterback will call signals something like this: "Hut one . . . hut two . . . hut three." The ball, of course, will be snapped on the actual count of three. But a fast-thinking running back should begin driving off the mark on the "hut" sound that precedes the "three." This is a fractional margin, to be sure, but it can give you an edge.

A player who is not quite sure of his assignment will usually be slow to get moving, so this is something else for you to consider. As you take your stance, review the play in your mind, double check your own role and then be ready to drive when you hear the snap number called by the quarterback.

There is something else to remember about the start—you must explode off that mark the same way every time, whether you are to be the ball-carrier, a potential pass receiver or merely a decoy. Discipline yourself to get off as quickly as possible on every play. By doing this, you will not fall into the habit of loafing or going half-speed on those plays when someone else is carrying the ball. Make consistency of effort your motto. Make the defense think you are getting the ball—even when you're not.

The most common types of starts from the three-point and the semi-upright stance are:

The cross-over step, in which you cross one leg over the other in the direction you intend to run and, in the same motion, pivot on the ball of the other foot. For example, in starting to your right, cross the left leg over the right leg, pivoting on the right foot and placing the left foot in the direction you intend to run.

The direct step, in which you start with the foot nearest the direction you intend to run. Example: if the play calls for you to run forward in a straight line, take a short step with your lead foot, driving off full speed on your second step. If you intend to run at an angle to the right side, then your lead foot points in that direction as you move out.

In all starts, try to take short, choppy steps instead of long strides. This will help your quickness off the ball and will give you better body control. You can lengthen your stride once you get through the hole or around the end. You need these short steps for quicker change of direction when picking your way through a small opening in the line.

THE BALL EXCHANGE

The importance of the ball exchange between quarterback and running back cannot be overemphasized. It is often the difference between winning and losing. A great blocking team, weak on ball-handling, may often have a sustained touchdown drive of 50 or 60 yards short-circuited by a sloppy handoff, a bobble or, worse yet, a fumble.

As with everything else in football, a smooth exchange is possible only if you and the quarterback work at it constantly in practice. A crisp exchange doesn't just happen out there on the field—it is the result of long hours of

Jim Butler (33) of Falcons makes quick change of direction through line.

drilling that develop timing and coordination between members of the offensive backfield.

There are, of course, various ways for the running back to take the ball from the quarterback during the exchange. But for purposes of brevity, let's look at the two most widely used techniques.

Near hand down: In this method, the hand nearest to the quarterback is held next to your hip with the palm facing up and the fingers spread fairly wide in position to grab the ball as the quarterback slaps it into your mid-section. The opposite arm is held in front of your chest, parallel to the ground and with the palm facing down. As soon as your near hand touches the ball, this opposite arm closes down over it to insure a more secure grip as you head into the line.

The main advantage of having your inside (or near) hand positioned back near the hip is shown when the quarterback has made his pivot a little slower than usual. If you had your hands out to reach for the ball, you would be past the quarterback before he could get the ball to you. By having your inside hand down, however, you form a pocket that will remain available to the quarterback almost until you are at the line of scrimmage. And this kind of mishap occurs quite frequently in a game, especially if you have a slow-turning quarterback or a runner who is very fast hitting into the line.

Your inside leg (the leg on the

same side that your near hand is waiting to receive the ball) should always be on a backward stride when you are taking the ball from the quarterback. To put it another way, the hip on which you are receiving the ball must not be coming forward at the moment of the exchange. A good back with high knee action is apt to knock the ball out of the quarterback's hands if he comes in with the inside leg and hip moving forward.

Some coaches drill their backs in this exchange by having them take the ball from the quarterback just as they would on a quick-opening dive play—only they must take the ball with only one hand, the inside (or near) hand. This drill helps the timing of the exchange and also serves to build confidence in the players involved in the exchange. Once you realize you can receive the ball with only one hand—well, you should be convinced that you'll never miss it with two hands during a ball game.

Elbow Up: This is the other type of exchange used in both college and professional ball. In receiving the ball, you should have your elbow nearest the quarterback (the inside elbow) raised almost shoulder high with the forearm parallel to the ground. The away hand is placed across the belt with the palm turned upward;

it must be held in this position— out of the way—until the ball has been placed in your mid-section.

There is an inherent danger in this exchange. If the near elbow is allowed to drop, it closes the pocket to the quarterback and might possibly jar the ball loose from his hands as he tries to place it in your mid-section. So keep that inside elbow *up.* Don't drop it until you feel the football against your belt buckle. That's the time to bring the elbow in tight—not before!

In any exchange, it is not necessary for you to rivet your eyes on the football as the play starts. Run your route the way you are supposed to, holding your hands and arms in the proper position, and trust the quarterback to get the ball to you. Don't reach for it or grab for it. Once you feel the ball in your stomach, squeeze it with both hands and protect it as much as possible while you hit into the line. There's a lot of traffic when you run inside and it's no place to use a fancy one-hand grip. Protect against a fumble at all costs. Remember that most football games between teams of relatively equal strength are won or lost as a result of turnovers—fumbles, interceptions, blocked punts, etc.

Reduce the number of turnovers and you'll be a winner! ●

The Challenge Of Running

One of the attractive aspects about running the football is that it gives you a certain freedom of expression and choice that is not available to most other players on the field.

True, there are many mechanics you are obliged to master (as we have seen in the previous chapter) and there are assignments that govern your movement to some degree. But the delight of being a ball-carrier is that you can often escape the restrictions and fly free, relying more on your instincts than on formations and systems.

This is a feeling that no one can appreciate unless he has taken the football from the quarterback, cut behind his pulling guard and broken into the open. It is pure exhilaration, a dizzying sensation of being alone and yet surrounded by enemy tacklers. There is that momentary glimpse of open daylight and you sense, in that moment, that you have broken the shackles that bind the other players to each other and to the ground. It is all there before you: the blockers clear a running alley inside the end, the defense is moved out of your path, a gap opens in the line and, beyond that, the end zone. A moment like this, to most backs, is worth all the work, sacrifice and punishment.

Teamwork, of course, is essential to a consistent running attack. A sound game plan, heads-up play selection by the quarterback and good blocking can give the ball-carrier the initial edge. In the final analysis, however, it is your instinct, your native ability and your desire (sometimes called "second effort" when it applies to a running back) that decides the issue. Good coaching and hard work in practice can prepare you for the test of running the football but inevitably it comes down to you as an individual against the other team as a unit. Winning

Gale Sayers (40) of the Bears was a back with style, speed and power.

touchdown runs can be diagrammed all day on the blackboard but they seldom work that way in game situations. The difference is that you can't diagram human desire and reaction and instinct with a piece of chalk.

From high in the stands or on the television screen, a running play looks clean, neat and well planned, with every man moving through his assigned steps. On the field, though, it looks quite different. It is a shifting pattern of bodies, big men jammed into close quarters. Openings are hard to see, and often they close a split second later. To the running back, every avenue seems obstructed by a guy wearing enemy colors. A field 100 yards long and 55 yards wide can suddenly become as small as a telephone booth when you have the football tucked under your arm.

As Detroit Lions' running back Mel Farr said in a previous chapter: "You know that you've got the ball and that wherever the ball is, that's where the crowd is going to be."

This is part of the burden of being a running back but it also part of the joy. Once the quarterback slaps the ball into your stomach, you become the focal point of everyone on the field, especially the opposing defense. You control the game in that instant; you govern the ebb and flow of play; you decide the tempo and rhythm of two entire teams. Your decisions, your movements determine everything.

Great running backs respond to this instant with brilliant individual effort. Good running backs trace their practice steps and hope the play will work as planned. Lesser players fail to seize the moment and crack under the pressure.

If you do not have exceptional natural skills and running instinct, you may never become a "great" running back. There have been only a handful of truly *great* ball-carriers down through the years anyway. But, with hard work and dedication, you can probably sharpen what skills you do possess to the point where you are a good ball-carrier. A coach cannot help you become great but he can make you an effective all-around backfield performer. He can provide you with the tools you need. Then it's up to you to use them.

Not all the pro backs listed among the top ten rushers in the NFL each year were "naturals" when they started. Fellows like Steve Owens of Detroit, Ken Willard of San Francisco, Marv Hub-

Marv Hubbard (44) of Raiders made himself a top runner through determination.

bard of Oakland and Ed Podolak of Kansas City began with only average physical ability. They got to where they are only through determination and a fierce desire to excel.

If you feel that you lack this total commitment, perhaps you'd better try another position. The demands made on a running back are too severe. Anything less than an all-out effort will waste your time and the time of your coaches and teammates. Many youngsters are lured to the backfield because they think it's a glamorous job. This is the wrong mental approach. Oh, there is glamour and excitement and the glory of scoring touchdowns. But these are only the end result of long and difficult preparation and self-sacrifice.

Take a tip: look at the negative side of being a running back before you consider the positives, and then decide if you really want the job.

Even if you feel you have exceptional natural talent, don't try to rush the learning process in the beginning. It has been pointed out in this book that one of the faults of young players is impatience; too often they want to look and act like All-Americans even before they've learned how to put on their shoulder pads. You are young. Give it time. And, again—

master the fundamentals of your position, be it end or tackle or halfback, before you think about inventing your own style of play. Gale Sayers, the former great Chicago Bears' running back, invented his style, and so did Jimmy Brown, the onetime Cleveland star. But they were exceptions to the rule. As a starter, you'll be better off modeling yourself after some of the running backs who came up the hard way—through diligent practice and guts, determination and close adherence to what their coaches taught them about carrying the football.

One of the first lessons you will learn, if history holds true, is that for every heart-pumping touchdown run you make, there will be a hundred carries where you are flattened at the line for a yard or two gain, if that. For every end sweep that breaks you into the clear down the far sideline, there will be several losses in your own backfield. For every crucial first down you make with that short tough yardage, there will be another try where you come up inches short—probably with a big defensive tackle sitting on your chest!

But, if you truly want to be a running back, you will gladly accept these challenges. The rewards are worth the investment. ●

Willie Ellison (33) of Rams makes a perfect cut behind his blocker.

Ball-Carrying Basics

■ Although running is mostly instinct and reaction, it also involves common sense and the application of certain proven techniques. You should be familiar with these basics before you start worrying about individual style.

The proper stance has already been discussed, as has the right way to get off the ball and the correct method of taking the handoff. Now it is time to consider what you do once you have the football under your arm.

The thing *not* to do, of course, is drop it or fumble it or juggle it as you head into the line or around the end. Once you take the ball from the quarterback, be it on a direct handoff, a pitchout or a forward pass, it is your responsibility to keep possession of it no matter what happens. This is not always possible. Football is a tough, rugged contact game and even the best runners have the ball jarred loose from time to time. What you want to avoid is losing

Fumbles are less likely to occur when the football is carried correctly.

it through carelessness. It's one thing to fumble after a clean, hard tackle; it's quite another to drop the ball because you have failed to grip it the right way.

The first bit of advice is: make sure you get the ball from the quarterback before you do anything else. Don't concentrate so hard on the hole opening in the line that you forget the mechanics of the exchange. If the exchange is smooth, at least you'll have the ball securely in your possession as you move toward the defense.

A secure grip on the ball is achieved by tucking it firmly into your ribs. The palm of the ball-carrying hand is placed over the forward part (or nose) of the ball with the fingers spread around the

point. The protective arm and elbow should be pressed close to your body. The other arm is used to give you balance in running and also to ward off tacklers.

Now quite probably you have seen college and professional backs carrying the ball loosely in one hand as they maneuver in the open field. This is not something you should try to copy, at least not at this stage of your career. It's best to have the ball tucked firmly to your body, particularly when you are running into the line, where the traffic is heavy and where there is a greater danger of having it knocked out of your hands.

More experienced runners can vary their grip on the ball, but for the time being, stick with the accepted method. Don't take chances. If you do, you may earn a reputation as a fumbler, a guy with "bad hands."

Before a running back breaks loose for big yardage, two things must happen. First, deceptive faking by the quarterback and the other running back. Second, effective blocking by the offensive line. A smart ball-carrier will help himself by keeping these two factors in mind as the play develops.

The action of the faking back will have a definite effect on your course of action. The fake is intended to not only fool the defense, but also to "freeze" it. This means causing the defensive linemen and linebackers to have a split second of uncertainty. While they are trying to figure out who has the ball and where the play is aimed, the offense has a momentary advantage. If you have a mental picture of what your teammates are doing on the play, you can better react to the moves made by the defense. You can time your moves to achieve the maximum effect from the deception.

Kyle Rote, a legendary receiver with the New York Giants for many years, said he could "see" the deceptive moves of his teammates while he was running a pass route down the field. He couldn't see them, of course, because everything was happening behind him. Still, his awareness of the various fakes enabled him to anticipate how the defensive men in front of him were likely to react. Kyle spent many hours learning the assignments of the entire backfield so he could put this knowledge to use to help him get open on his pass routes.

Before leaving the subject of backfield faking, it should be mentioned that you will be expected to carry out your fakes when someone else is running the ball. Many young players lose interest unless they are carrying the ball; they make a half-hearted effort at the fake and fail to follow through. Don't fall into this habit. Drive as hard without the ball as you do with it. Help your running mate when it's his turn to carry; you'll need his help when your number is called on a subsequent play. Remember, *winning football is a team effort.*

Effective faking is a result of conscientious practice habits. Work hard at this area of play during the week. If you are the decoy man on a running play, drive toward the quarterback just as if you're supposed to get the ball. Fake the exchange, pull your arms into your body as if you have the ball and hit into the line as hard as you can. Try to carry all fakes at least five yards beyond the line of scrimmage. This adds to the overall deception of the play. You may lack the ability to be an All-American runner but there's no reason why you can't be an All-American faking back.

A running back is only as good as his blockers. This is something you should never forget. Unless those guys up front do the job, your chances of advancing the ball are slim indeed. It's a fact that most great running backs play for teams with fine blocking lines.

The coordination between ball-carrier and blockers requires timing and discipline. As the runner, you can't be too anxious to hit the hole; you've got to train yourself to wait until the blockers, whether they are guards, tackles or halfbacks, can get into position to block their assigned defensive men. There's no sense rushing to the point of attack only to discover that your offensive linemen have not had time to do their job.

On quick-opening plays like dives and traps, the blocking is a bang-bang proposition. It either works or it doesn't, and there's no time for the runner to wait for the hole. It is a different story, however, on sweeps and other wise plays. Here the running back must be guided by the speed, direction and effectiveness of his blockers.

The cardinal rule on this type of play is to keep the required distance between yourself and your running blocker(s). If you run up his back or crowd him, you are only hampering yourself by narrowing down your running lane. This is a mistake made frequently by young inexperienced ball-carriers. In their anxiety to get up to the line, they angle in too sharply and thus reduce the effectiveness of the blockers. Your coach will give you the proper depth to keep on end sweeps and other outside plays, and you must work hard to keep this distance. Don't give in to the temptation to hurry things. This will only spoil the timing of the play.

In time you will find that you are developing a "feel" for the blocking up front. You will be able to gauge your speed to coincide with the pattern of the offensive line blocking. It will help too if you study the physical characteristics of your linemen. Some may pull more quickly than others on a wide play, and this means you may have to accelerate faster on your upfield cut. If a lineman is slower to reach the blocking area, then you must delay until he has gotten into the most favorable position.

Remember that sheer speed is not the answer to good running— at least not as the play is developing in the backfield. What you need here is a sense of timing. Larry Csonka of the Miami Dolphins is not a speed back but he gained over 1,000 yards in 1971 and 1972. How did he manage this? First, by making maximum use of his blockers and second, by not hurrying his upfield move until his blockers had gotten out ahead of him and cleared a running lane.

Many young ball-carriers make the mistake of trying to be open-field runners before they reach the open field. That is, they take the handoff and race toward the line, often arriving there before the blockers can clear running room for them. Sometimes it's better to be a little slower, particularly on end runs and sweep plays that require more time to develop.

Once you cut behind your blockers and get through the hole you can turn on the speed. You'll need it then to outrace those fast defensive backs in the secondary. But once again—you don't have to be a sprinting champion to be a smart running back. Work on that "feel" and that coordination with your blockers. Give them a chance to do their job before you do yours!

Even in the open field, though, sheer straightaway speed won't solve all your problems. Most linebackers and defensive backs today are picked for their speed, too, so you can't always count on out-

Floyd Little (44) of Denver follows interference on end sweep.

running them when you are fortunate enough to clear the line of scrimmage. Oh, there are times, of course, when you can turn on that after-burner and leave them in your wake. But not always. To be a complete running back you must also learn change of pace. Most of the great pro ball-carriers—Floyd Little of Denver is one who comes immediately to mind—have the ability to run at three or four different speeds. You think they are moving at top speed and, BANG!, they shift into high gear and race past you. When it appears that they are running at three-quarter speed, it's really half-speed. The defensive back hoping to make a tackle in the open field, is kept off balance by a ball-carrier who shows this change of pace technique.

Many runners are naturally gifted at using the change of pace; it's pure instinct with them. This does not mean, however, that you can't learn change of pace. You can! Work on it during practice. Run toward a tackler at three-quarter speed and wait for him to commit himself. When he makes his move, turn on full throttle and try to cut away from him at an angle. By the same token, you may want to run full speed toward the defensive man and then slow down a bit to force him into the first move. Try every-thing and see what reaction your various changes of speed will cause in the tackler. After a while you will begin to make these acceleration and deceleration changes without planning them in advance.

Here's an important tip: good running is a matter of being aware of the distance between you and the defensive man. If he is five yards away on a direct line, you may do one thing; if he's ten yards away coming at you from the side, you may try something else. You will come to recognize these distance gaps in time and your reaction will be almost automatic.

The same applies—as has been mentioned—to your blockers. Don't crowd them; give them room, and time, to carry out their assignments.

When a defensive man maneuvers you into a tight spot where you can't take evasive action, you can always use the side step and straight arm tactic. The straight arm, to be effective, must have the arm extended forward and locked at the time of impact. Extend the arm just before reaching the tackler and attempt to get to one side of him. If the tackler is met head-on, his momentum would carry him right through your straight arm. Place the heel of your hand against his headgear

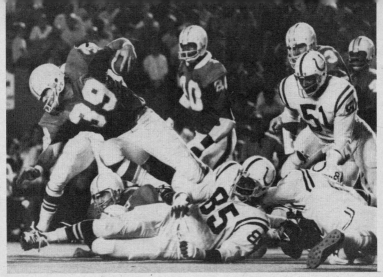

Miami's Larry Csonka (39) lunges for "second effort" yardage vs. Colts.

and, at the same time, take a sharp step to the side. Give your inside leg to the tackler and then, just as he makes a lunge, let your leg go limp until the tackler's deflected lunge has carried him beyond you. Finish the side step by bringing your near leg forward.

There is one cardinal rule that applies to every running back: *always get to the yardstick.* Make that first down before you do anything else. Never retreat.

Sometimes inexperienced ballcarriers get so involved with changing pace, weaving and cutting that they forget their first responsibility is to *advance the football.*

In time you will learn to work in tandem with your blockers in the open field. The trick is to make the defensive man commit himself in your direction so that your blocker can get a good angle on him. This is known as "setting a man up." Again, this requires some discipline and patience on your part. You can't afford to make your move away from the tackler too early—or your blocker will not be able to get good position on the defensive man. Learn to judge the reactions of defensive players when you are running toward them in practice. This will prepare you for actual game conditions where helping your blocker get his man will, in turn, help you to run to daylight.

A final reminder on running the ball: you may get away with brilliant individual efforts on occasion but usually your effectiveness as a ball-carrier will depend on the teamwork, aggressiveness and desire of the ten men playing with you. •

The Back As A Blocker

■ Although modern football has become a game of specialists, there are very few "running specialists." To play the offensive backfield today, you still must learn to block and to receive. These are as much a part of your job as carrying the football. This is particularly true of boys playing on the sandlot and high school level.

The more things you can do to help your team win, the more likely you are to make the team.

In its most elemental form, football is a game of body contact. It is man against man down in the dirt. This is what blocking is all about—you against him, and usually down in the dirt.

A coach can easily tell if a boy has the desire to play football by the way he blocks. This is one of the truest tests of a player. If a youngster shies away from the body contact of blocking, it's a good bet he will fail in other areas of the game too.

Blocking is as much a state of mind as it is a physical act. To be

a good blocker—and every running back should *want* to be a good blocker—you must convince yourself that there is nothing more important in the world than knocking that defensive man flat on his back. Most blocks, naturally, are not this decisive but your intent should never waiver: Run at him. Hit him. Drive right through him. Take him out of the play any way you can, but *take him out!*

As a running back, you should appreciate the value of good blocking. Your success depends on it when you are carrying the football. So, when another back is running the ball, you must make a concerted effort to carry out *your* blocking assignment. Technique is important in blocking. But sheer desire is more important. If you are determined to get at least a piece of your man, the chances are that you will. If you approach the job with something less than complete determination, it is likely that you'll fail.

Generally speaking, there are

Jim Kiick (rear) follows block by Dolphin teammate Larry Csonka (39).

Pass blocker (R) steps forward with inside leg and keeps head up.

Blocker drives into defensive man's chest and tries to straighten him up.

three types of blocks that a running back must learn to execute:

1. Blocking on a lineman, end or linebacker.
2. Blocking in the open field.
3. Pass blocking.

BLOCKING ON A LINEMAN

Blocking an inside lineman as the interference for a running play calls more for desire than technique. The idea here is to run straight at the defensive man you are assigned to block and drive him to one side or the other with your shoulder. In such close quarters, there isn't much room for either of you to maneuver, so this boils down to muscle on muscle, with determination the ultimate factor.

This type of block is usually required on a quick-opening play—a dive play on an inside trap—and so in many cases all you have to do is get your shoulder into the defensive man and wheel him out of the way. If you can't budge him, or he succeeds in stalemating your charge, at least screen him out of the play—that is, keep your body between him and the ball-carrier.

BLOCKING ON THE END

Most often a running back is asked to block on a defensive end

Pass-blocking rule: hit your man once, hit him again—and stay with him.

or a linebacker on outside running plays.

The technique for this type of block varies, of course, but there are some accepted guidelines:

Get off the ball fast and build up speed as you near the defensive end or linebacker. You want him to take more punishment than you do.

Go directly at him but try not to let him know whether you intend to take him out or whether you are merely going to fake a block on him.

Aim for the spot he will be at when you meet him. After a couple of plays, you should be able to tell what kind of an end he is, and

you can plan your blocking charge accordingly. He may be a crasher, a waiter, a floater, or he may be all three. Size him up early in the game.

Just before making contact, work for good blocking position—but don't lose your momentum!

Hit him with abandon. Jolt his ribs with your shoulder to the side of the play and *run right through him.* If you fail to make solid contact, at least stay with the defensive man and screen him out of the play.

When you encounter an end or linebacker too big and tough to handle with your normal shoulder block, *go after him low.* Shoot your body across his knees and continue rolling into him until he goes down.

OPEN FIELD BLOCKING

This type of block is more difficult from the two just described because the defensive man is in the open and has more room to elude your blocking attempt. It is absolutely necessary to maintain good balance. Run at your man fairly low for better body leverage, using short, choppy strides. Keep your head up, your eyes straight ahead and your arms close to your body. Move at maximum speed on a line that will enable you to intercept the defensive man, but run under control so you can alter course if he changes his direction.

Don't commit yourself too soon in the open field. Close in on the defensive man and then *block right through him.* Repeat: *block through and not just to the man.* Make contact and drive him back or to the side, anywhere just so long as you keep contact and don't let him slip off the block. Avoid the mistake of throwing yourself bodily at the defender from too great a distance. It's safer to keep your feet under you in case you miss the block; at least this way you can pursue him and perhaps nail him the second time around. The crossbody or reverse body blocks are beautiful to see but extremely difficult to execute in the open field.

You can improve your open field blocking technique by watching the defensive man's belt buckle instead of his head or eyes. This will keep you from being fooled by his fakes.

You have one big advantage as a downfield blocker. You know where the play is going—or is supposed to go—so you anticipate the defender's moves because he is trained to go for the man with the football. Knowing the course of the runner and the defensive man's pursuit angle, you can mentally plot a point of interception.

Your responsibility as a block-

ing back does not end when you knock your man down in the open field. Hustle back to your feet and look for another defender to hit. Never give up trying to knock someone down until the whistle blows to end the play.

Desire and pursuit. Pursuit and desire. This is what makes a good open field blocker.

PASS BLOCKING

A passing attack is only as

Robert Holmes of Chiefs (45) gets good blocking on this end run.

good as the passer, and the passer is only as effective as the blocking provided by his backs and linemen. In other words, unless the quarterback has time to throw, the aerial game will be minimized by the defense.

As a backfield man, you form a secondary blocking barrier for the passer. The offensive linemen are in the forward trenches; their job is to hit the enemy along the line and blunt his pass rush. Your assignment is to "pick up" any linemen who penetrate this forward screen, or linebackers who may blitz or red-dog on the passing down. You have an advantage over your lineman in that you are stationed behind the line and there is no defender immediately in front of you on the snap.

Your primary responsibility as a pass blocker is to *step toward the line of scrimmage as the ball is snapped.* This step must be taken with the *inside leg*. This forward stride with the inside leg lessens the area between you and the defensive pass rusher by a yard or two, depending on the length of your stride and the defensive man's speed. It also gives you solid position to protect the inside alley. Your outside leg is drawn back and is poised for the sharp turn to the outside in the event a defensive rusher breaks through from that direction.

Since backs are usually smaller and lighter than the defensive linemen and linebackers they must take in pass blocking situations, they must rely on good initial position (the forward step with the inside leg) and deception rather than sheer strength to do the job.

Think of yourself in terms of being a zone blocker—that is, you are protecting a certain zone in front of the passer; you are not looking for any specific defensive man to block. You take the first defensive player who appears in or near your zone. It could be a tackle crashing up the middle or a linebacker coming on an outside red-dog rush. In either case, you wait for the defensive rusher to come to you. You never go chasing him. Remember, you have that zone to protect in front of the quarterback. If you move away from this area, you'll leave a

hole in the protective blocking pocket.

When you are pass blocking, crouch a little, flexing the knees, and keep your head up and your eyes straight ahead so you can see where the rush is coming from. As your man comes toward you, raise both forearms in front of your chest and, using an uncoiling motion with your knees, come up into him, chest to chest. The idea on this first move is not to knock him down but merely to pull him up short, to delay him on his path to the quarterback. Your job is not finished with this initial contact. You should recover as quickly as possible, keeping your feet under you for maximum balance, and pop him a second time and, if necessary, a third time. Whatever happens, keep after your man. Keep between him and the quarterback. Delay him any way you can.

Some backs will attempt to low-cut the pass rusher by throwing a body block across his knees. This is okay—*IF* you get him. If you miss, however, it's a simple matter for him to hurdle over your prone body and nail the quarterback. Use the low-cut block only as an extreme measure. You are always more useful to your quarterback if you keep on your feet.

Pass blocking, in the backfield

Forty-Niner blockers cleared this gaping hole for FB Ken Willard (40).

or along the line, is a physically exhausting thing, so use your head as much as possible. Don't try to overpower those big linemen. Finesse them if you can. Don't get involved in hand-to-hand tussles; it takes too much out of you. Get into your man quickly with a sharp jolt and then use footwork to set up and hit him again. It doesn't matter how the block looks, just as long as you don't let him get to the passer.

As you acquire more experience in the pass blocking, you'll probably develop your own techniques. It's a good idea, for instance, to vary your style. Hit the pass rusher sharply one time, then wheel him to the outside the next time. Keep him guessing as to what type of block you may use next.

If you get a chance to see the New York Giants play, either in person or on TV, watch fullback Charlie Evans when quarterback Norm Snead drops back to throw. Evans, a big fellow at 6-3 and 220 pounds, is a crushing pass blocker who really pops any defensive man who breaks through into his area.

Another of the NFL's top pass blocking backs is Ken Willard of San Francisco. Larry Csonka and Jim Kiick give the Miami Dolphins two big, strong backs who can deal out punishment to rival pass-rushers.

Copy the techniques of these famous pros if you can but remember that the thing that makes them great pass blockers is that they *want* to block. This is desire. ●

The Back As A Receiver

■ One of the chief reasons for the explosive offenses in modern football is that running backs have become almost as adept at catching forward passes as the ends and flankers.

Years ago, running backs were used primarily for two things: 1) carrying the ball on running plays, and 2) blocking. But to be a running back today you must have the ability to catch passes. Maybe you don't have to be as big and strong as the tight ends who catch those short tosses over the middle or as fast as the 9.3 wide receivers who go deep for the "bomb." But you must be able to catch the ball.

Catching the football out of the backfield requires, in addition to natural ability and good hands, *desire, concentration* and *lots of practice.*

You may recall that in the previous chapter it was pointed out that you can become a good blocker only if you *want to block.* Well, the same applies to pass receiving. When the football is in the air, you must want to catch it more than any other player on the field. In that split second, catching the pass must be the most important thing in your life. This, again, is called desire.

Concentration is vital to pass receiving. When you run a pass route out of the backfield, you must not let anything distract your attention from the flight of the football. Don't sneak a look at the man covering you at the last second. Never take your eyes off the ball once you have focused on the pass. Nothing else should matter to you except making the reception.

Many young receivers make the mistake of trying to watch both the defender and the ball at the same time. True, you must watch the defensive back while you are running your route and trying to elude him. Once you turn to look for the ball, though, forget everything else. Pretend you are all alone on the field and the ball is spiraling towards you and there's no reason why you shouldn't

John Fuqua of the Steelers is one of top pass-catching backs in NFL.

catch it and run for a TD.

Running backs are not required to run as many different kinds of pass routes as, say, a wide receiver or a flanker back. Your primary job is still to run the football. Still, pass receiving is an important function and so you will do well to study your routes carefully and practice them as often as you can.

If you are an accomplished receiver—as many pro running backs are—your value to the team will be increased tremendously. You will pose a double threat to the defense, which means your quarterback can use you in a variety of ways.

Catching a football, for the most part, is a natural thing. Most boys know how to catch. But you can improve yourself by constant practice, by learning your individual routes and by studying the various defenses you must run them against. It won't matter a darn that you can catch the ball if you can't get open in the secondary to provide a target for the passer.

In most cases, routes out of the backfield are shorter than those run by ends and flankers. There are circle routes over the middle, flares and "safety valves" to the flat zone, screens, sideline routes and buttonhooks. These routes may be known by different ter-

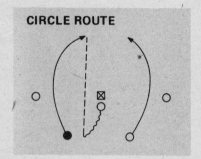

CIRCLE ROUTE

minology but they are easily recognizable from the accompanying diagrams.

Because they are usually shorter in length, backfield pass routes do not require flat-out speed. What they do call for is timing, deception and a change of pace. You need not be reminded that these very same traits are necessary when you run the ball.

Walt Garrison of the Dallas Cowboys is a running back who is feared as a pass-catcher, as is little Mike Garrett of San Diego.

As a young running back, you should attempt to copy the style of some of these outstanding professional stars. Watch them use head fakes, delays and instant acceleration to get open. And take note of their *complete concentration* on catching the football, even when they are in tight spots with defensive people all around them.

This latter point is the key to receiving passes out of the backfield. In most instances, you will not find yourself wide open in

128

some thinly-protected zone. More likely you'll be catching the football "in a crowd," as they say. This takes more than concentration. It takes guts. You hear those big linebackers thundering down on you and you feel their breath on your neck, and yet you can't afford to take your eyes off the ball. You know you are likely to get hit—and hard—the moment you touch the ball but if you are a good receiver, you put everything out of your mind except one thing: *catch that ball!*

Make an all-out effort to catch any ball thrown to you, even those which appear hopelessly out of your reach. Extend yourself. You may be surprised how many catches you can make with this extra bit of determination.

This is something you can work on in practice. Have the quarterback throw the ball over your head, off to one side and down at your feet. It's a good drill for him, throwing to spots, and it will help you get accustomed to grabbing passes that are not right on target. After all, this is what you must often do in a game when the quarterback is under pressure as he throws and you are being hounded by a defensive player as you attempt to make the catch.

Coaches can devise plays and diagram them on the blackboard and perfect them in practice but only desire and determination will make a play successful on the playing field.

CATCHING THE FOOTBALL

Passes should be caught with just the hands whenever possible, with no effort to use the arms or body as aids in holding the ball. The hands and wrists should be

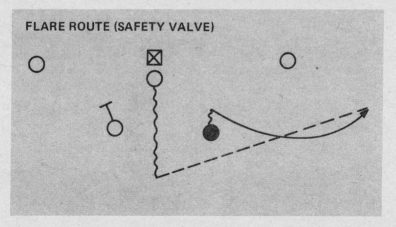

FLARE ROUTE (SAFETY VALVE)

relaxed and loose, with the fingers spread comfortably wide. The receiver must keep his eye on the ball once he has committed himself to make the catch.

In general, passes above the chest should be caught with the thumbs pointing in, whereas passes below the chest should be taken with the thumbs pointing out. There is one exception to this rule—when the ball is being taken over the shoulder on the dead run. In this case, the thumbs should be pointing out. As the ball touches the hands they should give slightly, much in the manner of a baseball player's hands as he catches a hard line drive. The slight give of the hands acts as a sort of shock

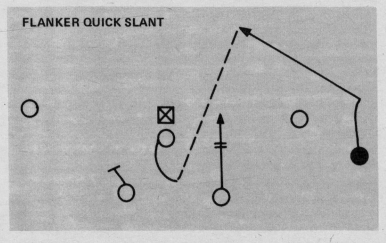

FLANKER QUICK SLANT

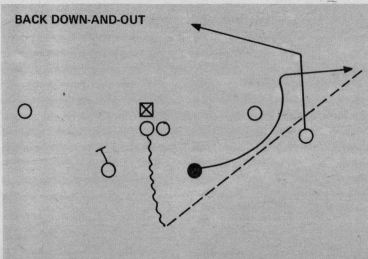

BACK DOWN-AND-OUT

absorber. The receiver should not extend his arms until the last second; premature extension will cause loss of rhythm in the stride.

Deception plays a major role in the routes run by backfield men. Usually, your route will come off a play action fake. This is when the quarterback fakes a running play into the line to "freeze" the defense and then throws to one of his running backs. As you will learn from your coach, you must add to this deception by playing out your part to the hilt, whether it requires a fake block, a fake handoff or a decoy pass route to the opposite side of the gridiron.

This gets back to the theme of teamwork. Unless every man on the squad carries out his assignment, the success of the play will be questionable. You must act out of unselfishness, placing your personal thoughts and actions second to those of the team. If your fake into the line, or your decoy route to the flat, succeeds in pinning down one single defensive player, well, you have been instrumental in making the play work.

Several years ago, an NFL team lost its chance at the league title because a halfback did not carry out his fake pass route, and the defensive man assigned to cover him dropped off into another area and made an interception that turned the game right around. The halfback was promptly traded.

The lesson here is clear: approach every play as if you were going to carry the ball or catch the ball. Make your movements realistic. Play it for keeps—even when you don't have the football under your arm.

There is a saying that "you play football the way you practice football," and again the message is obvious. You develop your tempo and rhythm during the week, not on game day. Put everything into your practice sessions. Discipline yourself to run hard on every play, to fire out on your fakes or decoy routes. Punish your body by driving for ten yards when your coach requires you to run only five yards past the line of scrimmage. Don't cheat yourself by trying to cut corners. If you are half a football player on Wednesday or Thursday, you cannot except to be a complete player on Saturday or Sunday. Bad habits are not shaken that easily.

Since this chapter has dealt with the running back as a pass receiver, it might be good to repeat that you can excel in this department only if you have *a burning desire to catch the football.* Speed, deception, good hands, guts . . . these will all help make you a good receiver. But only if you start with the one indispensable ingredient—desire! •

Mike Garrett (20) of Chargers follows blockers on classic end sweep.

Running Plays And Their Use

■ In this day and age of multiple offenses, there are literally hundreds of running plays that can be used within a dozen different formations. And yet these are no more than take-offs or variations of four of the game's oldest and most fundamental plays:

1. The off-tackle power play.
2. The end sweep.
3. The inside trap.
4. The quick-opener.

There's no intent here to attempt to diagram and explain a long list of running plays. These differ to such a degree, depending on formation, personnel and coaching preference, that such an undertaking would be impractical. But it won't hurt to take a look at the four basic plays and their place in overall offensive strategy.

In each instance, the accompanying plays have been drawn up against defensive alignments common to high school and college football—the 6-3-2, the 5-3-3 and the 5-2-4. The editors believe that these defenses are those faced most often by players in the age group at which this book is aimed. The professionals, of course, see mostly 4-3-3 defenses, but this is another story.

OFF-TACKLE POWER VS. 6-3-2

The off-tackle power play is based more on fundamental blocking and teamwork than on the usual T-formation deception. It is a valuable play in short-yardage situations when your side must retain possession of the ball.

As shown in Diagram A, the off-tackle play to the halfback employs massed blocking at the point of attack, the gap between the defensive left end and left tackle. There are a pair of double-team blocks used here. The left guard and the fullback combine to wipe out the defensive end, driving him toward the outside. Meanwhile, the offensive right end and tackle team up to force the defensive tackle to the inside. If these blocks are successful, there is a good running lane opened up for the halfback.

You may recall that in an earlier chapter, the factor of timing by the ball-carrier was discussed at length. Well, here's where that timing pays off. After taking the handoff from the quarterback, the running back starts laterally toward the right. He stays on this course while the blockers up front move into position to carry out their blocking

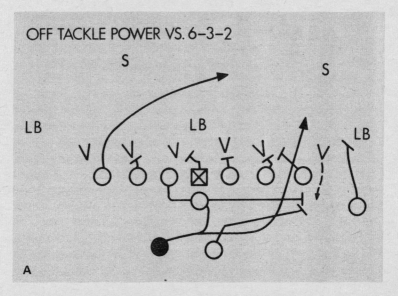

OFF TACKLE POWER VS. 6-3-2

A

STRONGSIDE END SWEEP VS. 5-3-3

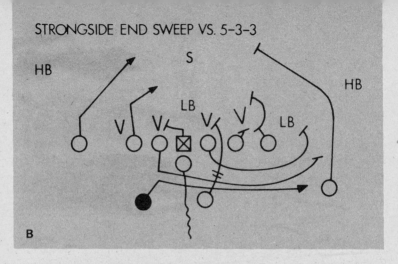

INSIDE TACKLE TRAP VS. 6-3-2

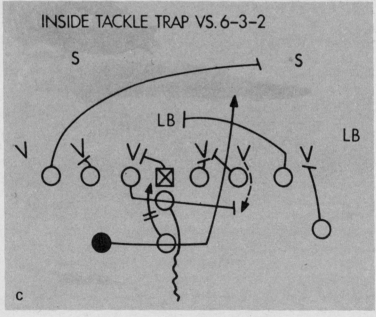

assignments. As the blocks are put on the defenders, the halfback sees the opening outside his tackle and quickly changes direction, turning straight upfield and racing through the hole before any of the opposing players can slip their blocks. If the ball-carrier cuts upfield too soon, the hole may not yet be opened; if he delays a second longer than needed, the hole will be closed by the time he reaches the line of scrimmage. Only playing experience will teach you the "feel" of this kind of a running play.

Another reminder: when you study your playbook, make an attempt to learn the roles of the other men on your team. In this manner you will be more familiar with what is supposed to happen up front on plays like the off-tackle power. If you can visualize the overall play as it is developing, you have a better chance of making yardage.

END SWEEP VS. 5-3-3

The classic end sweep illustrated in Diagram B is a wide-open running play that can get your team big yardage in a hurry—that is, if you have a runner fast enough to turn the corner plus a pair of cat-quick pulling guards. This is a play that will make a running back appreciate the value of the boys up front.

The success of this sweep depends on two factors: 1) the quarterback's initial fake to the fullback, which is intended to make the defense react to an inside running thrust and, 2) the speed of the ball-carrier and the pulling guards in getting good position to the outside. The guards must pull quickly from their positions and run laterally along the line of scrimmage. Their job is to get to the outside and seal off any de-

fenders in that area. The right guard gets the enemy linebacker; the left (or offside) guard takes the first defender he sees.

The ball-carrier's chief responsibility is to take the handoff (after the quarterback fakes to the fullback) and to begin a wide sweep to the right, running parallel to the line of scrimmage rather than toward it until he sees that the guards have gotten out there and have sealed the defenders to the inside. Once he clears the blocking area, the ball-carrier just turns on the speed and heads down the sideline.

The end sweep is not quite the play to call when it's third down and one, since there is a risk of losing yardage in a play that develops so deep in the offensive backfield. But as a potential long-gainer, say, on first down around mid-field, it's a great call. It's the kind of a play any running back likes because it gives you an opportunity to shake free of the line and do your stuff in the open. It's a "run to daylight" play.

INSIDE TRAP VS. 6-3-2

Diagram C shows a running play that is almost as old as the game itself, the inside trap—in this case, a tackle trap. This play is usually called when: 1) the quarterback has successfully run a regular off-tackle power play several times and senses that the defense is set up for the trap, and 2) when the defensive tackle is changing in hard and exerting pressure on the offensive line. A trap play that clicks is one of the prettiest sights in football.

The inside trap is just what the name implies—a play designed to lure a defensive lineman while the ball-carrier slips through the area just vacated by the defender.

As shown in Diagram C, the offensive left guard and tackle angle to the left to put a double-team block on the defensive guard. This leaves the defensive tackle completely free, and he rushes into the backfield. Just as he clears the line of scrimmage, however, the offensive left guard, who has pulled from his position,

comes crashing into him from the side (the trap block) and drives him to the outside. The ball-carrier, meanwhile, times his up-field cut to coincide with the trap block and races through the gap left by the defensive tackle when he made his charge into the back-field.

This play is particularly successful against younger, over-zealous defensive linemen who try to pressure the offense on every play. After he's been trapped a few times, though, the defensive man usually becomes a little wiser and more cautious.

QUICK-OPENER VS. 5-2-4
The fullback quick-opener shown in Diagram D might also be

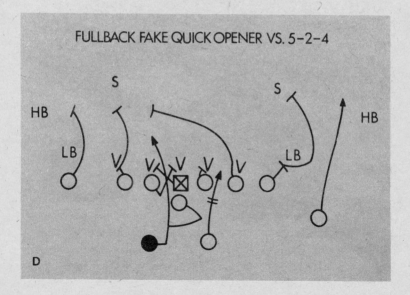

FULLBACK FAKE QUICK OPENER VS. 5-2-4

D

Les Josephson (34) of Rams has three-man escort on this end run.

called a "fullback counter." A counter play is one which starts to one side, and suddenly shifts back in the opposite direction, hoping to catch the defense going the wrong way.

As the diagram shows, the quarterback spins quickly to his right and fakes a handoff to the halfback, who drives hard into the guard-tackle hole on that side of the line. If this fake is convincing enough, the defense is likely to make its initial reaction toward the halfback. The fullback, meanwhile, also takes a jab step to the right, adding to the illusion that the play is indeed going that way. Just as quickly, however, he veers back to the left, takes the handoff and hits to the left side of his center.

The quick-opener is very effective against a defense such as 5-2-4 since there are no linebackers in the middle. Once the fullback clears the line, he's in the open. This is a play that can get you a quick two yards—or a quick 40 yards, depending on the ball-carrier's speed.

The four plays used as illustrations in the chapter all have several things in common. They require split-second timing by the ball-carrier and quarterback, deception to "freeze" the defense and effective blocking up front. If one of these ingredients is missing, well, you'll find the yardage tougher to get. If two of these ingredients are missing, you'd better have some extra desire. You'll need it. •

How The Pros Run It

■ Some of the outstanding ball-carriers in the National Football League came into the game with their own distinctive style of running the ball; others succeeded in copying the style of someone else, perhaps even improving on it.

As a young running back, you should watch the professionals in action whenever possible, not necessarily to imitate them but more for the general lessons to be learned by observing the men who have developed ball-carrying to a fine art.

Actually, running the football requires more instinct than anything else. There are some mechanical techniques, some predetermined moves, but usually a good running back acts out of instinct. He will make a move here, a cutback there, and yet he won't be able to say why he made these specific moves. In most cases, they "just happen."

There are, naturally, different kinds of running backs and, where possible, you should watch the fellows who have something in common with your style of running. For instance, if you are a small, fast outside runner, there's not much sense trying to model yourself after someone like Steve Owens of Detroit or Larry Csonka of Miami, both of whom are big, bruising inside power runners. You'd be better off concentrating on Larry Brown of the Redskins, Mike Garrett of San Diego or John Fuqua of the Pittsburgh Steelers. They are all fast, shifty outside runners, more on your style.

The pro scouts generally rate Csonka, Owens, Willard, John Brockington of Green Bay, Willie Ellison of Los Angeles, Calvin Hill of Dallas, MacArthur Lane of Green Bay, Franco Harris of Pittsburgh, John Riggins of the Jets and Marv Hubbard of Oakland as the top power runners in the NFL. These are the fellows called on when their club faces a "must" third-and-one situation.

Although Brockington and the others mentioned above are full-back types, they are not the stereotyped fullback of yester-

Miami's Larry Csonka is rated one of the top power runners in pro ball.

year. These men are big enough to power inside the tackles but also fast enough to break off those long-gainers. Brockington went 52 yards for the Packers on a short-yardage dive play, and Ellison reeled off an 80-yard touchdown run for the Rams, the longest running play in the NFL in 1971.

Owens, the former Oklahoma All-American, is one of the genuine pluggers in pro ball. He gained 1,035 yards for Detroit in 1971, averaging 4.2 yards a carry—and he got most of his yardage the hard way, banging head-first between the tackles, spinning and digging for every inch. Steve is not a classical runner as far as form goes but he certainly gets the job done.

Two of the most sensational outside runners in the NFL are 5-9 200-pound Mike Garrett of San Diego and 5-11 200-pound Johnny Fuqua of Pittsburgh. As you can see, neither of these players is a giant by modern backfield standards. But they have fine outside speed.

Fuqua and Garrett and others before them, men like Jon Arnett, the onetime Rams' running great, have proved that there is definitely a place for the "little man" in pro football. Lack of size can be a handicap, to be sure, but it can easily be offset by sheer speed and burning desire to run the ball. Use these players as a model if you are a boy who feels he is not big enough or heavy enough to be a running back.

Most pro running backs are so talented that they have the speed to go outside plus the strength and drive to run inside as well. Ron Johnson of the Giants fits into this category, as do Altie Taylor of the Lions, Larry Brown of the Redskins, Floyd Little of the Broncos, Leroy Kelly of the Browns and O.J. Simpson of the Bills.

There is a striking similarity between Larry Brown of Washington and the Giants' Ron Johnson. They are stylish runners with a smooth stride and the ability to accelerate from one step to the next. Change of pace is one of their favorite weapons, too. Both men have several different speeds and they keep the defense constantly off balance by shifting from one gear to another.

Floyd Little may be one of the most underrated running backs in NFL history. Floyd seldom gets the headlines reserved for Larry Brown, but he is a 1,000-yard rusher, a back who specializes in the "big play" for Denver. Floyd was a tireless workhorse for the Broncos in 1972, carrying the ball 216 times for a 4.0 average. Whenever Denver got in a hole, they handed the ball to their 5-11 195-

John Riggins of the Jets uses speed, bruising power to get yardage.

pound running back. It was almost automatic.

Injuries have slowed Leroy Kelly of the Browns somewhat in recent years, yet he remains one of the league's most dangerous all-around backs. Leroy is a smart runner; nine years in the NFL have taught him all the tricks of carrying the football. He can instantly adapt his speed and power to a situation on the field. Like the other great runners, Kelly has explosive acceleration. Usually it takes only one block to spring him free around the end; from there, his jet takeoff sends him down the sideline.

O.J. Simpson, a Heisman Trophy winner at USC, came into pro ball heralded as one of the finest runners in collegiate annals—and he has not disappointed, despite being with a losing team in Buffalo. Simpson is primarily an outside runner but he's a threat inside too and he's also a dangerous pass-receiver coming out of the backfield.

O.J. finally fulfilled his potential in 1972 when he gained 1,251 yards on 292 carries—a 4.3 average—to win the NFL rushing title.

As was pointed out in an earlier chapter, modern running backs must also be capable pass-catchers. They must pose a dual threat to the defense.

Among the pros, it is generally agreed that the best receivers among the running backs are Walt Garrison of the Cowboys, Ron Johnson of the Giants, Donny Anderson of the Cardinals, John Fuqua of the Steelers, Jim Kiick of the Dolphins and Mike Garrett of the Chargers.

Garrison, a player-coach with Dallas, and Kiick are the players to study if you want to know how to run pass routes out of the backfield. They rely more on technique and knowledge of the defenses rather than on outright speed. Opposing linebackers are usually no match for Garrison and Kiick in one-on-one situations.

If you go back over this chapter on the top pro running backs, you'll discover that there are all kinds of styles and sizes and speeds represented. This should prove to any young running back that he doesn't have to be this big or that fast; all he must have is some natural ability to carry the football. The rest will take care of itself. ●

The Pass Receiver

Thoroughbred of the Game

■ The offensive end is the Thoroughbred of a football team—sensitive, high strung, fleet of foot, flowing movement, hidden power. In a game founded on savage body contact and played by huge men with broad shoulders and tree-like thighs, the modern pass-catcher is an individual easily distinguished from his muscular confederates. There is a lean greyhound look about him, a look that suggests speed and grace and an elegance not always evident in other football players.

In the aesthetically beautiful act of catching a sideline pass or splitting two defensive backs over the middle, the receiver sometimes resembles a matador making a classical pass against an enraged bull. There is a sureness in his movement, almost an air of contempt. There is a delicate touch with the hands, a nimbleness with the feet. The offensive end needs such qualities. He lives in the secondary by his wits and his style rather than by brute strength and raw power. He plays the game with his feet, his fingers and his eyes. He is a con man in the shell game of the gridiron. He is the darting, elusive hare with the yelping defensive hounds always in hot pursuit.

Because he is the "other half" of modern football's exciting guided missile show, the offensive end is vitally important to any team that hopes to achieve victory on Sunday afternoon. Although most coaches will insist they strive for a perfect balance of running and passing, and that offensive football cannot be successful without the consistent ground attack, it is accepted that the fastest, easiest and most effective way to score points is by "putting the ball in the air," as Y.A. Tittle was fond of saying. The home run bomb to Fred Biletnikoff or Otis Taylor or Lance Alworth is the great equalizer. It is the game-buster and the crowd-pleaser. Defeat becomes victory when a Don Maynard or a Paul Warfield makes an over-the-shoulder grab on the dead run and goes all the way. One electrifying pass play involving Willie Richardson or Bob Tucker or Gene Washington or Harold Jackson or Dick Gordon or Gary Garrison can make an entire season.

Although the offensive end is not usually constructed along the same lines as a hulking tackle he still must possess a certain toughness. Life is

Fred Biletnikoff (25) of Raiders is one of game's best clutch receivers.

not always tranquil in the deep zones and sometimes the graceful matador is gored by the frustrated bull. The pass receiver heading downfield must be alert for a "clothesline" shot by the corner linebacker. When he catches the ball there is not always room to display his sprinter's speed; in such uncomfortable instances he can expect to be battered and pounded by angry linebackers and fast-moving defensive backs. He is seldom treated gently after making a reception. The defense tries to soften him up, hoping that perhaps he might be "listening for footsteps" the next time around. The pass catcher is actually paid to avoid contact whenever possible but he must be prepared for it every time he runs a pattern down the field. He is, in fact, blessed with extra-ordinary courage since he must give his undivided attention to the flight of the football, often leaving himself vulnerable to savage blind-side tackles. The good ends can, as they say, catch the ball in heavy traffic. This means in the short zone, over the middle, where the defense converges suddenly and savagely on the man going for the ball. There is no game of will-o-the-wisp here; it is collision-course contact, brutal and punishing. The end no sooner wraps his hands around the ball than he is buffeted from two sides. The jarring force of such tackle rattles his teeth and sets off sirens inside his helmet. Momentarily, the high-strung Thoroughbred with the legs designed for speed becomes a rugged quarter horse built for heavy duty.

The real ends usually hold on to the ball no matter what—for this is their assignment. Touchdowns come later but first—catch that ball! ●

Catch That Ball!

■ Football today, even on the sandlot and high school levels, has become somewhat of a guided missile show. Strong-armed quarterbacks launch the missiles and sure-handed receivers flag them down in the recovery zone. Together they form the game's most exciting and electrifying combination.

The forward pass is to football what the home run is to baseball—a bolt of lightning, an instant score, a crowd-pleaser.

As Hall of Fame quarterback Y.A. Tittle was fond of saying during his days as a star with the New York Football Giants: "Running the football is okay but, as for me, I like to put the ball in the air. That's the quickest, easiest and most sensible way to score."

No quarterback, however, even a great passer like Tittle, can effectively "put it in the air" unless (or until) he has someone to catch it. That "someone" might be an elusive flanker back, a swift split end or a rugged tight end. He might be tall or he might be short. He might be a "fly boy" or a plodder. But he must always possess two qualities—the *ability* to catch the ball and the *desire* to catch the ball.

It's difficult to say which of these two is more important. A boy with the ability but not the desire can never hope to be more than a mediocre receiver. The player who possesses burning desire but poor physical co-ordination faces a similar fate. A happy combination of the two would seem to be the best formula for success as a pass catcher.

As has been pointed out in previous chapters, ability can be improved, to a degree, in a young player; indeed, sometimes it can even be taught. But no one, high school freshman or veteran professional, can be programmed for desire. The great running backs in football are those with the desire to fight for the extra yard or two. Likewise, the best receivers are those who want to catch the ball more than the defensive man wants to prevent them from catching it.

If an athlete has desire, it follows naturally that he also has a high degree of confidence—and confidence, is a characteristic found in all top pass receivers.

Jerry Smith of Redskins (87) goes high to grab game-winning TD pass.

They are able to convince themselves that they *will* catch the ball, no matter where it's thrown and no matter how tough the defensive coverage might be. The thought of *not* catching the ball rarely occurs to them. It is, in a sense, a form of positive thinking. An end or flanker back who is gripped by any kind of doubt as he takes his stance at the line of scrimmage or in the backfield immediately lessens his effectiveness as a receiver. Without realizing it, he is playing right into the hands of the defense—because he has allowed uncertainty to creep into his mind and this will surely have an effect on the way he runs his pass route and how he reacts to defensive pressure.

Of course, no receiver—even the great pro stars—can catch every ball thrown in his direction. Sometimes the quarterback throws the ball poorly and it bounces in front of the receiver or else sails far over his head. Sometimes the defensive back collides with the receiver as they both go for the pass, and the ball is jarred loose or deflected. And, as everyone who has played the game well knows, there are those embarrassing occasions when the receiver simply drops a pass that has been thrown right into his hands. No one can explain why or how this happens, but it does. And that's what makes football such a great game; despite all the modern technology, despite all the computers and playbooks and scouting firms, despite all these things, it is still the unpredictable human element that determines whether a play works or not.

Ask most football coaches what they look for in a pass receiver after they have looked for desire and ability and in a majority of cases the answer will be "intelligence." Offensive end is a "thinking man's" position. It requires split-second computing and the ability to recognize defenses. It calls for a player who is mentally one step ahead of the opposition, an athlete who can temper his quick, slashing routes with precise, calculated moves. Because the offensive end is often split far out from the main battle on a football field, some people have the impression that he is detached from the central team effort, a lonely sentry cut off from the flow of the game. Nothing could be farther from the truth. A heads-up end is very much involved in every play, be it a pass or a run, and this involvement requires him to be aware of many things: blocking assignments, backfield fakes and play action, the routes being run by other receivers and, of course, defensive reaction. This is why a receiver must be a player with intelligence and alertness, a player whose mind and senses work as quickly and deftly as his hands and feet.

An end who is running a pass route down the field should be aware of everything that is going on *behind* him. If he knows what fakes are being carried out in the backfield, what blocking is taking place in the interior line and what other pass routes are in progress, well, he can better determine what overall effect the play is having on the defensive team. This knowledge is invaluable in helping him carry out his individual role in the play.

Good hands—that is, the feel and touch required to catch a football—are important in the make-up of a pass receiver. More important, perhaps, than sheer speed. It doesn't matter how fast a receiver is if he drops the ball after speeding downfield to catch it. This is why many coaches look for good hands before they begin considering speed and size in an end candidate. Of course, a coach is always delighted to discover a young fellow who has good hands *and* speed, not to mention size.

Bob Hayes of the Dallas Cowboys, the "world's fastest human," is a pro end with size, speed and good hands. So are Gene Washington of the San Francisco 49ers, Paul Warfield of the Miami Dolphins, Harold Jackson of the Philadelphia Eagles, Otis Taylor of the Kansas City Chiefs,

Gene Washington of 49ers makes sure on this lunging catch in end zone.

Great moves, rather than speed, help Dan Abramowicz of Saints get open.

Charley Taylor of the Washington Redskins, John Gilliam of the Minnesota Vikings, Rich Caster of the New York Jets and Gary Garrison of the San Diego Chargers.

But outright sprinter's speed isn't absolutely necessary. A receiver who utilizes intelligence, mistake-free pass routes and clever moves can be just as dangerous as a fellow who runs the 100-yard dash in 9.3 or thereabouts. There are many examples of this type of receiver in the NFL. Fred Biletnikoff of the Oakland Raiders, the 1972 AFC pass catching champion, is one. Fred is no speedburner but he manages to get himself open because he runs terrific individual pass routes, because he uses lots of savvy when he starts operating in the secondary, and because he has exceptional hands. When it comes to footracing, Fred probably would finish second to a lot of guys around the league; when it comes to getting free for a crucial third-down reception, though, the Oakland star is almost in a class by himself.

Don Herrmann of the New York Giants, Dave Parks of the Houston Oilers, Dan Abramowicz of the New Orleans Saints, Chip Myers of the Cincinnati Bengals, Jack Snow of the Los Angeles

Rams and Ron Sellers of the Dallas Cowboys are other outstanding pro receivers who fall into a similar category. They all have a certain amount of speed, naturally, but more often they rely on skill and experience to get open in the secondary. Herrmann, the young Giant star, may be one of the best route-runners in pro football.

Although the receiver can be more of an individual in his play during a game than, say, an offensive guard, he is still part of a two-man team (he and the quarterback) and so he must develop coordination, timing and "feel" with the passer. This sense of teamwork can be achieved during practice and especially in games, where things are done under competitive pressure. But it always takes time. Two players just don't learn each other's moves overnight.

Perhaps the heaviest responsibility for this phase of passer-receiver cohesion rests with the quarterback, whose task it is to sense when his receiver may be deviating from a predetermined route in an effort to get open. A sudden and unexpected change of speed and direction by the end means the quarterback must alter his throwing motion and quickly deliver the ball into another area. Likewise, if the passer comes under a strong rush by the defensive line and is forced to release the ball sooner than he had planned, the receiver must make adjustments in his original route and try to "break it off," as they say, in an effort to provide the quarterback with an immediate target.

The ability to run with the football after making the catch is present in most outstanding receivers. The fellows who can turn a simple 10-yard zig-out pattern into an explosive 60-yard touchdown run are coveted by coaches on all levels of the game. But most coaches will agree that this ability is secondary. The receiver's main task is still to *catch the football.* This comes before all else and it should be uppermost in the receiver's thinking every time he lines up. Catch the football first—and *then* worry about making a touchdown. The only exception to this rule occurs on a third-down situation. Then it is imperative that the receiver not only catch the ball, but also that he advance it at least as far as the yardstick that will give his side a first down. There's no use running an eight-yard square-out when you need 11 yards for the first down.

It's easy to see why an end must always be alert and aware of such things as down and yardage, field position and time left to play. ●

Gary Garrison (L) of Chargers shows determination in making this catch.

A Must:
Good Hands

■ Catching a football is very different from catching any other kind of ball. And the reason is obvious: in the rugged, fast-moving contact sport of football there is always someone physically trying to prevent you from making the catch. This means that fellows who play the pass receiving positions in football must have more than just good hands; they must also possess a fierce desire to catch the ball, no matter what the consequences, plus strength, sturdy legs, keen eyesight and the ability to concentrate on the ball without "hearing footsteps."

All great receivers have good hands, flexible, "soft" and with a fingertip sensitivity for handling the football. Some athletes are born with this gift; it comes naturally to them. Other players must work hard to develop the "feel" necessary to become an outstanding pass catcher.

Before a receiver starts to concentrate on such things as pass patterns, cuts, fakes, reading defenses, etc., he should learn to catch a football softly—that is, without fighting it. Fingers, hands, wrists and arms must be firm and yet relaxed at the moment of the catch. Watch some of the top pro receivers—players like Fred Biletnikoff of Oakland, Gene Washington of San Francisco, Otis Taylor of Kansas City, J.D. Hill of Buffalo, Ben Hawkins of Philadelphia—and you'll notice that they almost seem to absorb the football as it comes to them. At the moment of the catch, their arms "give" like sensitive coil springs and thus the impact of the ball hitting their hands is softened considerably.

Of course, different types of passes require different handling by the receiver. A short, hard ball cannot always be caught softly, especially when the receiver is running at a sharp angle to the passer. Likewise, it is often difficult to let the arms and hands "give" when the ball is thrown below the knees. Young pass catchers must learn to make adjustments for the various types of passes that might be thrown to them during a ball game. It is not always possible (or advisable) to attempt a "textbook catch" of a badly-thrown pass. The main thing is to get the ball anyway you can, even if it doesn't look fancy, and worry about form later on.

The practice field is the place for the young receiver to learn about catching the football. There he can run the various routes required of his position and begin to develop an idea of how and when the ball will be coming to him, angle, height, speed and so on. He will learn, for example, that there is quite a difference between catching a high, floating lead pass down the field than there is hanging on to a quick sideline bullet. He will learn that it is more difficult to get into a favorable receiving position on a sharp zig-out move than on a standard slant-in.

All good pass catchers make a supreme effort to get every ball thrown in their direction. This is the motto by which they live. No ball is too low or too high or too far away for them to get.

Although the art of catching a football is often a thing of individual style and skill, there are certain fundamental rules which most coaches and receivers adhere to. Here are some of them:

- While running a pattern, the receiver should carry his hands about chest high to facilitate getting them up or down in a hurry, depending on where the ball is thrown.

- Don't start reaching for the ball too soon. This has a ten-

The correct hand and arm position for catching an over-the-shoulder pass.

dency to reduce running speed.

- If the receiver is traveling in the direction of the flight of the ball, he should attempt to catch it over his shoulder with his palms facing in, thumbs out, elbows bent and arms slightly extended from his body.

- The receiver must keep his eye trained on the football at all times, concentrating only on the pass, and disregarding any opponent who might be defending against the play.

- Always keep your body between the defensive man and the ball.

- When the pass is under-thrown, the receiver should make an extra effort to return and catch the ball.

- If a defender has him covered closely, the receiver should not wait for the ball to settle into his hands. He should reach back and try to pluck it out of the air. (Note: this is not the same as reaching for the ball too soon, a point which was made earlier in this chapter).

- It is the receiver's duty to see that the ball is not intercepted—that is, if he has any kind of a chance on the play. He should deflect the ball or bat it away from any defensive player if he can't catch it himself, and if he sees that the opposition is in a position to intercept it.

- The receiver's first duty is to *catch the ball.* His second task is to run with it. He should avoid the mistake of trying to run with the ball *before* he has caught it.

On this latter point, there are several NFL receivers who are also outstanding ball-carriers once they have caught the football. John Gilliam of the Minnesota Vikings averaged 22.0 yards in 1972 while Gene Washington of San Francisco averaged 20 yards each time he received a pass. Both did it mainly on speed, as did Rich Caster of the New York Jets, whose 21.4 average was tops in the AFC.

Body control has much to do with good receiving. A pass catcher must strive to maintain good balance during the act of running his route and while attempting to catch the ball. If he is running too fast—or out of control—he will be unable to alter his direction or change his body position to compensate for a poorly-thrown pass. The perfect pass is one that allows the receiver to take the ball in full stride without having to stop or slow down, but

it doesn't always happen this way, and so the receiver should move under control and with good balance so he is prepared to make instantaneous adjustments in acceleration, direction and depth.

Olympic-type speed, like that possessed by Bob Hayes of the Dallas Cowboys, is an asset to a receiver only when he learns to combine it with balance and control, plus a change of pace.

One thing young receivers should keep uppermost in their minds is this: most defensive backs today are just as fast as the pass catchers. Coaches pick their defensive backs on the basis of speed, quickness, agility and reaction. There are almost as many 9.5 sprinters playing defense in college and in the pro ranks as

QBs and receivers should get use to each other in practice drills.

Receiver should learn to catch all kinds of passes in practice.

there are at the receiving positions. What does this mean to a receiver? Well, it means that he can't count on beating his defensive man on speed alone. Rather he must learn to employ a change of pace. He also must vary his routes and his moves so that he keeps the defensive man off balance and guessing. Once or twice during a typical ball game—well, maybe three or four times—a split end or a flanker will be asked to run a deep fly pattern down the sideline. This is probably the only route where a sprinter can really open up and turn on full throttle. Most other times he is assigned routes that require not speed but finesse and timing and, as mentioned, a change of pace.

There are times, too, when sheer speed can be a detriment to a team's passing attack. Remember, outside of the NFL, there aren't too many quarterbacks

with the arm or the accuracy to hit a receiver who is sprinting down the sidelines 40 or 50 yards away. A receiver must always judge his position in relation to the quarterback. There's not much point in racing 60 yards down the field when you *know* that the passer doesn't have the strength of arm or, which is more often the case, the time to throw the football that far.

The conclusion to be drawn here is obvious: young receivers (and young quarterbacks, too) would be wiser to concentrate on perfecting their short pass patterns—the ones they will have to use most often in a ball game—instead of practicing the touchdown "bomb," a pass which is difficult to complete under the most ideal conditions and which is very often dangerous and foolhardy to even attempt. As Miami quarterback Bob Griese, says:

"The longer a football is hanging up there in the air, the more bad things (interceptions) can happen to it."

It is not unusual for quarterbacks and receivers to remain on the field *after* practice to work on specific moves that need polishing. For example, the receiver may be having trouble with his timing on the tricky sideline square-out move. The only way to perfect this individual route is for the quarterback and the receiver to work on it constantly during practice and after practice, whenever they have the time. They can also critique each other's moves. The quarterback, for instance, might say to the receiver: "I don't think you're planting your inside foot firmly enough just before you make the outside break." Or the receiver might point out to the quarterback: "Maybe this thing would work better if you released the ball a split second sooner; I have the feeling I'm waiting on the ball after I make my break."

Practice is also a good time for the receiver to improve his skill at catching poorly-thrown passes. He can ask the quarterback to make him come back for an underthrown pass, or leap for a high throw, or dive for a low ball. This is good training because he will be expected to catch similar off-target passes in a ball game—when it really counts.

A good pass catcher also must learn, somewhere along the line, how to recover his balance—or even get back up off the ground—after the defensive team has jolted him or knocked him off stride during his route. The first rule here is never give up on the ball. A lot of touchdowns have been scored by receivers who looked like they were completely out of the play—but who showed enough determination to get back to their feet, pick up the pass pattern (or improvise a new one) and catch the ball.

There are "tricks of the trade," so to speak, that most young receivers learn by experience and through sound coaching.

In summary, catching a football is part desire (determination), part natural skill, part speed, part intelligence and part fundamentals. Most young players can catch the football well enough to become adequate receivers, provided they have the other necessary qualities as well. But to become an outstanding pass catcher, someone like Paul Warfield of the Miami Dolphins, well, that takes a little extra. It takes pride, a special sense of timing, dedication to a goal and, above all, long, hard hours on the practice field catching the football. ●

Getting Open

■ It's one thing to have the ability to catch a football. It's quite another thing to get open so you have a chance to use that ability.

Basically, there are three ways for a pass receiver to get open against a tough pass defense:

1. Sheer speed.
2. Faking, feinting or changing direction.
3. Change of pace.

The matter of sheer speed has been discussed at length and it is generally agreed that, while this gift is certainly not one to be overlooked, a good receiver must combine speed with the ability to fake and a change of pace if he hopes to establish any consistency at all. Occasionally a receiver will find that he can beat the man covering him by the simple expedient of out-running him down the sideline. In that case he can probably use his natural speed to get open and catch the football. More often, though, the receiver must employ other techniques to shake free of his defender.

But before getting into the business of speed and faking and change of pace, it might be good to review two fundamentals which are indispensable to all pass receivers. One is stance; the other is the release.

THE STANCE

On the high school and college levels, most receivers line up in the accepted three-point sprinter's stance. In professional football, the wide receivers (split end and flanker) usually start from a standing (or upright) position while the tight end assumes the three-point stance. In the three-point stance, the receiver drops either his left or his right foot several inches to the rear and uses the hand on that same side as the third point in the stance. His back is fairly level, his head is up, eyes straight ahead. He tries to keep his weight slightly forward so that he will be able to push off and accelerate quickly once the ball is snapped. On the snap, he drives off the rear leg, pumps his arms hard and stays low for several strides until he has built up a good head of steam. If he straightens up immediately, he is in danger of losing whatever forward momentum he might have been able to generate by driving (or pushing) off the back leg. You might have noticed that sprinters in track lean into their start for several yards before straightening up.

Another advantage of the three-point stance—in addition to aiding a quick getaway—is that it puts the receiver at the right height to block an opposing lineman or linebacker, if that's what his role in the play requires him to do. This is why the tight ends in the NFL all use the three-point stance; they do much of their team's blocking, and it's almost impossible to throw an effective block from a standing position.

Wide receivers, on the other hand, are rarely asked to do any serious blocking—and so they can afford to line up in a standing position. One reason for this position is that it enables them to look over at the quarterback and thus pick up his audible signals better. Also, it gives them a chance to scan the secondary and to determine what kind of defense they may be running into once the ball is snapped.

Whatever stance the pass receiver uses, however, he must be alert and ready to explode off the mark as fast as possible and to avoid being held up on the line by the enemy. A receiver is of no use to his team if he is unable to work his way into the open where the quarterback can see him and get the football to him. That's why it is so important for all receivers to learn how to release from the line of scrimmage.

THE RELEASE

The tight end is more likely to be held up at the line by an opponent than a wide receiver, so he must work at various moves that will get him away from the line of scrimmage as quickly as possible. If a linebacker or a defensive end plays right on top of him and attempts to prevent him from running his route, the receiver can evade him in any one of several ways. He can throw a head fake to the inside, take a short jab step in that direction and then sprint to the outside before the defensive man recovers. He can also fake a block on the defensive man, making it appear as if a running play is developing, and then slide off the man and break into the secondary. When the defensive man is particularly tenacious in his efforts to hold the receiver on the line, the receiver can hit into the defender and spin away (or roll out). This is a tricky move, though, because it sometimes throws the pass catcher so far off course that he is unable to run his route as planned. The pivot-out is a very effective method of escaping from the clutches of a defensive player. The end takes a step with the outside foot slightly deeper than and parallel to the line of scrimmage, pivots completely away from the man trying to collar him, and sprints toward the sideline.

Once away from the line of scrimmage, the receiver's next job is to run his route (a *route* is the path run by a single receiver; a *pattern* consists of routes run by several receivers) and get open to receive the pass from the quarterback. This is where feinting, faking and change of direction come into the picture.

Head, shoulder and foot fakes should be utilized against a defender who can match the receiver's speed but who may not have his coordination or physical reaction. In other words, you can't out-run him but you might be able to out-fox him. No matter how you achieve this, the end result is the same: you get open to receive the pass—and that's a receiver's job. A smart receiver will soon learn that many fast defensive backs are defeated by their own speed; that is, they are so fast that they over-commit to the receiver's initial move and cannot recover in time to pick the man up again.

The purpose of a directional fake is to try to make the defender commit himself, physically and mentally, in one direction—at which instant the receiver breaks sharply in another direction. The idea is to catch the defender leaning one way and then gain a step or a step and a half on him by changing course. This kind of a complete body fake requires speed, body control and sudden acceleration. The key words here are "body control." There's no point in faking the defender, beating him cold with a great fake, only to fall down or stumble during the change of direction.

There is one general rule that applies to all fakes in the secondary. It is this: don't run in curves and circles. Break off every move sharply and then take the straightest, most direct line to the point you are trying to reach. Time and steps are precious when you are racing to catch the football. Make your cuts and veers decisively and crisply with as little wasted motion as possible.

Many young receivers confuse faking with change of pace. Actually, the two techniques are very different. The change of pace is precisely what the name implies— the receiver uses several different speeds in an attempt to fool the defensive back who is covering him.

If the defensive back is too hasty and obvious in his judgement of what *he thinks* you are going to do, he will often give himself away by overreaching or by anticipating your moves prematurely. If you establish a certain pattern to your moves early in the game, you will find that the defensive back assigned to you often falls into step with this pattern. When this happens—and providing you recognize it—you can take advantage of your man by utilizing some form of change of pace.

The next time you see an NFL game, notice how the good receivers vary their speed on certain pass routes. Some of the top pass catchers, in fact, may utilize three or four changes of pace on a single pass route. They start off at three-quarter speed, slack off to half-speed midway in the route, and then throttle up to full speed in an attempt to beat their man deep.

Although a receiver must often deviate from his planned pass route because of defensive pressure or some other unexpected development, young players should always strive to run the routes as they are outlined by the coaching staff. Each individual route is designed for a specific purpose within the overall pass pattern. Each individual route helps to set up the hoped-for completion. What one receiver does in the deep zone may well be the key that opens up a teammate for the completion in the short zone.

In sandlot and high school football, where the quarterback does not always have a lot of time because of poor blocking, he depends a great deal on his receivers running their routes the way the play calls for them to be run. He has a primary target and maybe a secondary target, and these are the two men he's looking for down the field. If one or both of these receivers decide to do a solo bit, the passer may not be able to locate them. And even if he can locate them, he may not be in the right position to complete the pass. What this means is that each and every receiver has a responsibility to the quarterback to try and be *where* he's supposed to be *when* he's supposed to be there.

It helps too if a pass receiver knows exactly what his fellow receivers are doing on a specific play. Since their moves are coordinated with his, it is important that he be aware of distance and spacing and timing for everyone in the pattern. Knowing what's happening on other parts of the field also enables a heads-up receiver to determine how the defense is being affected by the various fakes and by the general flow of the play.

And that, after all, is what pass receiving is all about. Run your route. Beat the defense. Get open. Catch the football! ●